CAMBRIDGE LIBRARY COLLECTION

Books of enduring scholarly value

Linguistics

From the earliest surviving glossaries and translations to nineteenth century academic philology and the growth of linguistics during the twentieth century, language has been the subject both of scholarly investigation and of practical handbooks produced for the upwardly mobile, as well as for travellers, traders, soldiers, missionaries and explorers. This collection will reissue a wide range of texts pertaining to language, including the work of Latin grammarians, groundbreaking early publications in Indo-European studies, accounts of indigenous languages, many of them now extinct, and texts by pioneering figures such as Jacob Grimm, Wilhelm von Humboldt and Ferdinand de Saussure.

The Rudiments of English Grammar

The English polymath Joseph Priestley (1733–1804) defined grammar as nothing more complicated than a system of rules for the correct use of language. This enlarged second edition of his influential 1761 textbook first appeared in 1769; it had by then established him as one of the major grammarians of his age. With little patience for the confusing and super-fluous application of Latin rules to English, Priestley champions a simple style of grammatical explanation here, questioning even such fundamental concepts as an English future tense. The text follows a clear question-and-answer structure designed for students. Priestley's determination to modernise the teaching of English and to promote usage as the crucial linguistic standard remain relevant today. A companion work, *A Course of Lectures on the Theory of Language and Universal Grammar* (1762), is also reissued in this series, along with other works by Priestley ranging in coverage from oratory to oxygen.

T0370943

Cambridge University Press has long been a pioneer in the reissuing of out-of-print titles from its own backlist, producing digital reprints of books that are still sought after by scholars and students but could not be reprinted economically using traditional technology. The Cambridge Library Collection extends this activity to a wider range of books which are still of importance to researchers and professionals, either for the source material they contain, or as landmarks in the history of their academic discipline.

Drawing from the world-renowned collections in the Cambridge University Library and other partner libraries, and guided by the advice of experts in each subject area, Cambridge University Press is using state-of-the-art scanning machines in its own Printing House to capture the content of each book selected for inclusion. The files are processed to give a consistently clear, crisp image, and the books finished to the high quality standard for which the Press is recognised around the world. The latest print-on-demand technology ensures that the books will remain available indefinitely, and that orders for single or multiple copies can quickly be supplied.

The Cambridge Library Collection brings back to life books of enduring scholarly value (including out-of-copyright works originally issued by other publishers) across a wide range of disciplines in the humanities and social sciences and in science and technology.

The Rudiments of English Grammar

Adapted to the Use of Schools;
with Notes and Observations,
for the Use of Those Who Have Made
Some Proficiency in the Language

JOSEPH PRIESTLEY

CAMBRIDGE
UNIVERSITY PRESS

CAMBRIDGE
UNIVERSITY PRESS

University Printing House, Cambridge, CB2 8BS, United Kingdom

Published in the United States of America by Cambridge University Press, New York

Cambridge University Press is part of the University of Cambridge.

It furthers the University's mission by disseminating knowledge in the pursuit of education, learning and research at the highest international levels of excellence.

www.cambridge.org
Information on this title: www.cambridge.org/9781108065887

© in this compilation Cambridge University Press 2013

This edition first published 1769
This digitally printed version 2013

ISBN 978-1-108-06588-7 Paperback

This book reproduces the text of the original edition. The content and language reflect the beliefs, practices and terminology of their time, and have not been updated.

Cambridge University Press wishes to make clear that the book, unless originally published by Cambridge, is not being republished by, in association or collaboration with, or with the endorsement or approval of, the original publisher or its successors in title.

THE
RUDIMENTS
OF
Englifh Grammar,

Adapted to the USE of SCHOOLS;

WITH

NOTES and OBSERVATIONS,

For the USE of Thofe

Who have made fome Proficiency in
the Language.

By JOSEPH PRIESTLEY,
LL. D. F. R. S.

A NEW EDITION, Corrected.

LONDON:

Printed for T. BECKET and P. A. DE HONDT, in
the Strand; and JOHNSON and PAYNE, in Pater-
nofter-Row.
MDCCLXIX.

[v]

T H E

PREFACE.

IN the firſt compoſition of the *Rudiments of Engliſh Grammar*, I had no
fartherviews than to the uſe of ſchools;
and, therefore, contented myſelf with ex-
plaining the fundamental principles of the
language, in as plain and familiar a manner as I could. Afterwards, taking a more
extenſive view of language in general, and
of the Engliſh language in particular, I
began to collect materials for a much
larger work upon this ſubject; and did not
chuſe to republiſh the former work, till I
had executed the other; as I imagined,
that this could not fail to ſuggeſt ſeveral
improvements in the plan of it. How‐

A 3   ever

ever, being frequently importuned to re-
publifh the former grammar, and being
fo much employed in ftudies of a very
different nature, that I cannot accomplifh
what I had propofed, I have, in this treatife, republifhed that work, with improvements, and fo much of the materials I had collected for the larger, as may
be of practical ufe to thofe who write
the language. Thefe materials, therefore,
I have reduced into as good an order as I
can, and have fubjoined them to the former grammar, under the title of *Notes
and Obfervations, for the Ufe of thofe who
have made fome Proficiency in the Language.*

I have retained the method of *queftion
and anfwer* in the *Rudiments*, becaufe I am
ftill perfuaded, it is both the moft convenient for the mafter, and the moft intelligible to the fcholar. I have alfo been fo
far from departing from the fimplicity of
the plan of that fhort grammar, that I
have made it, in fome refpects, ftill more
fimple; and I think it, on that account,
more fuitable to the genius of the Englifh language. I own I am furprized
to fee fo much of the diftribution, and
technical terms of the Latin grammar,
re-

retained in the grammar of our tongue ; where they are exceedingly aukward, and abfolutely fuperfluous ; being fuch as could not poffibly have entered into the head of any man, who had not been pre- vioufly acquainted with Latin.

Indeed, this abfurdity has, in fome meafure, gone out of fafhion with us ; but ftill fo much of it is retained, in all the grammars that I have feen, as greatly in- jures the uniformity of the whole ; and the very fame reafon that has induced fe- veral grammarians to go fo far as they have done, fhould have induced them to go far- ther. A little reflection may, I think, fuffice to convince any perfon, that we have no more bufinefs with *a future tenfe* in our language, than we have with the whole fyftem of Latin moods and tenfes ; becaufe we have no modification of our verbs to correfpond to it ; and if we had never heard of a future tenfe in fome other language, we fhould no more have given a particular name to the combination of the verb with the aux- iliary *fhall* or *will*, than to thofe that are made with the auxiliaries *do*, *have*, *can*, *muft*, or any other.

A 4　　　　The

The only natural rule for the ufe of technical terms to exprefs time, &c. is to apply them to diftinguifh the different modifications of words ; and it feems wrong to confound the account of *inflections*, either with the grammatical ufes of the *combinations* of words, of the *order* in which they are placed, or of the *words which exprefs relations*, and which are equivalent to inflections in other languages.

Whenever this plain rule is departed from, with refpect to any language whatever, the true fymmetry of the grammar is loft, and it becomes clogged with fuperfluous terms and divifions. Thus we fee the optative mood, and the perfect and pluperfect tenfes of the paffive voice, abfurdly transferred from the Greek language into the Latin, where there were no modifications of verbs to correfpond to them. The authors of that diftribution might, with the very fame reafon, have introduced the dual number into Latin ; and *duo hemines* would have made juft as good a dual number, as *utinam amem* is an optative mood, or *amatus fui* a perfect tenfe. I cannot help flattering myfelf, that future grammarians
will

will owe me some obligation, for introducing this uniform simplicity, so well suited to the genius of our language, into the Englifh grammar.

It is poffible I may be thought to have leaned too much from the Latin idiom, with respect to several particulars in the ftructure of our language; but I think it is evident, that all other grammarians have leaned too much to the analogies of that language, contrary to our modes of fpeaking, and to the analogies of other languages more like our own. It muft be allowed, that the cuftom of fpeaking is the original, and only juft ftandard of any language. We fee, in all grammars, that this is fufficient to eftablifh a rule, even contrary to the ftrongeft analogies of the language with itfelf. Muft not this cuftom, therefore, be allowed to have fome weight, in favour of thofe forms of fpeech, to which our beft writers and fpeakers feem evidently prone; forms which are contrary to no analogy of the language with itfelf, and which have been difapproved by grammarians, only from certain abftract and arbitrary confiderations, and when

A 5 their

their decifions were not prompted by the genius of the language; which difcovers itfelf in nothing more than in the general propenfity of thofe who ufe it to certain modes of conftruction. I think, however, that I have not, in any cafe, feemed to favour what our grammarians will call an irregularity, but where the genius of the language, and not only fingle examples, but the general practice of thofe who write it, and the almoft univerfal cuftom of thofe who fpeak it, have obliged me to do it. I alfo think I have feemed to favour thofe irregularities, no more than the degree of the propenfity I have mentioned, when unchecked by a regard to arbitrary rules, in thofe who ufe the forms of fpeech I refer to, will authorize me.

If I have done any effential fervice to my native tongue, I think it will arife from my detecting in time a very great number of *gallicifms*, which have infinuated themfelves into the ftyle of many of our moft juftly admired writers; and which, in my opinion, tend greatly to injure the true idiom of the Englifh language, being contrary to its moft eftablifhed analogies.

I dare

I dare fay, the collections I have made of
this nature, will furprize many perfons
who are well acquainted with modern compofitions. They furprize myfelf, now
that I fee them all together ; and I even
think, the writers themfelves will be furprized, when they fee them pointed out.
For I do not fuppofe, that they defignedly
adopted thofe forms of fpeech, which are
evidently French, but that they fell into
them inadvertently, in confequence of
being much converfant with French authors.

I think there will be an advantage in
my having collected examples from *modern writings*, rather than from thofe of
Swift, Addifon, and others, who wrote
about half a century ago, in what is generally called the claffical period of our
tongue. By this means we may fee what
is the real character and turn of the language at prefent ; and by comparing it
with the writings of preceding authors,
we may better perceive which way it is
tending, and what extreme we fhould
moft carefully guard againft.

It

It may excite a fmile in fome of my readers, to fee what books paffed through my hands at the time I was making thefe collections, and I might very eafily have fuppreffed their names; but I am not afhamed of its being known, that I fometimes read for amufement, and even any thing that may fall in my way. Befides, I think there is a real advantage in making fuch collections as thefe from books which may be fuppofed to be written in a hafty manner, when the writers would not pay much attention to arbitrary rules, but indulge that natural propenfity, which is the effect of the general cuftom, and genius of the language, as it is commonly fpoken. It is not from the writings of grammarians and critics that we can form a judment of the real prefent ftate of any language, even as it is fpoken in polite converfation.

It will be no objection to the propriety, or ufe of any of my remarks with thofe who think juftly, that they were fuggefted by the perufal of the writings of Scotchmen. It is fufficient for my purpofe, that they write in the Englifh language. Many

of

of their readers will not know that they were Scots. If they excel in other articles of good ftile, their example is not the lefs dangerous ; and he muft be prejudiced to a degree that deferves ridicule, who will not allow that feveral of the moft correct writers of Englifh are Scotchmen.

Some of my examples will be found without authorities, and many of them without references to the particular paffage of the author This was generally owing to mere inattention, in omitting to note the author, or the place, at the time I was reading ; and afterwards, the overfight was irretrievable.

I make no apology for the freedom I have taken with the works of living authors in my collections. Except a very few pages in Swift, I read nothing with an immediate view to them. This was always a fecondary confideration ; but if any thing of this kind ftruck me in the courfe of my reading, I did not fail to note it. If I be thought to have borne harder upon Mr. Hume than upon any other living author, he is obliged for it to the

great

great reputation his writings have juſtly
gained him, and to my happening to read
them at the time that I did ; and I would
not pay any man, for whom I have the
leaſt eſteem, ſo ill a compliment, as to
ſuppoſe, that exactneſs in the punctilios
of grammar was an object capable of giving him the leaſt diſturbance. This is
the ſmalleſt point of excellence, even with
reſpect to ſtyle ; and ſtyle, in its whole
extent, is but a very ſmall object in the
eye of a philoſopher.   I even think a man
cannot give a more certain mark of the
narrowneſs of his mind, and of the little progreſs he has made in true ſcience,
than to ſhow, either by his vanity with
reſpect to himſelf, or the acrimony of his
cenſure with reſpect to others, that this
buſineſs is of much moment with him.
We have infinitely greater things before
us ; and if theſe gain their due ſhare of
our attention, this ſubject, of grammatical
criticiſm, will be almoſt nothing.   The
noiſe that is made about it, is one of the
greateſt marks of the frivoliſm of many
readers, and writers too of the preſent
age.

Not that I think the bufinefs of language, and of grammar is a matter of no
importance, even to a philofopher. It is,
in my opinion, a matter of very confiderable confequence; but in another
view. That I have, accordingly, given
a good deal of attention to it, will, I
hope, appear by a *Courfe of Lectures on the
Theory of Language, and Univerfal Grammar*,
which was printed fome years ago for
private ufe, and which I propofe to correct,
and make public. To the fame treatife
I muft, likewife, refer my readers for the
fatisfaction I may be able to give them,
with refpect to the definitions of terms,
and fome other articles relating to Grammar, in which I differ from Mr. Harris,
and other grammarians.

With refpect to our own language,
there feems to be a kind of claim upon
all who make ufe of it to do fomething for its improvement; and the beft
thing we can do for this purpofe at prefent, is to exhibit its actual ftructure, and
the varieties with which it is ufed. When
thefe are once diftinctly pointed out, and
generally attended to, the beft forms of
fpeech, and thofe which are moft agreeable

able to the analogy of the language, will foon recommend themfelves, and come into general ufe; and when, by this means, the language fhall be written with fufficient uniformity, we may hope to fee a complete grammar of it. At prefent, it is by no means ripe for fuch a work; but we may approximate to it very faft, if all perfons who are qua-lified to make remarks upon it, will give a little attention to the fubject. In fuch a cafe, a few years might be fufficient to complete it. The progrefs of every branch of real fcience feems to have been prodigioufly accelerated of late. The prefent age may hope to fee a new and capital æra in the hiftory of every branch of ufeful knowledge; and I hope that the Englifh language, which cannot fail to be the vehicle of a great part of it, will come in for fome fhare of improvement, and acquire a more fixed and eftablifhed character than it can boaft at prefent.

But our grammarians appear to me to have acted precipitately in this bufinefs, and to have taken a wrong method of fixing our language. This will never be
effected

effected by the arbitrary rules of any man, or body of men whatever; becaufe thefe fuppofe the language actually fixed already, contrary to the real ftate of it: whereas a language can never be properly fixed, till all the varieties with which it is ufed, have been held forth to public view, and the general preference of certain forms have been declared, by the general practice afterwards. Whenever I have mentioned any variety in the grammatical forms that are ufed to exprefs the fame thing, I have feldom fcrupled to fay which of them I prefer; but this is to be underftood as nothing more than a conjecture, which time muft confirm or refute.

A circumftance which may give us hopes to fee the fpeedy accomplifhment of the defign of completing the grammar of our language, is the exceeding great fimplicity of its ftructure, arifing, chiefly, from the paucity of our inflections of words. For this we are, perhaps, in fome meafure, indebted to the long-continued barbarifm of the people from whom we received it. The words we afterwards borrowed from foreign languages,

guages, though they now make more
than one half of the fubftance of ours,
were like more plentiful nourifhment to a
meagre body, that was grown to its full
ftature, and become too rigid to admit
of any new modification of its parts.
They have added confiderably to the bulk
and gracefulnefs of our language; but
have made no alteration in the fimplicity
of its original form.

Grammar may be compared to a treatife of *Natural Philofophy*; the one confifting of obfervations on the various changes, combinations, and mutual affections
of words; and the other on thofe of the
parts of nature; and were the language
of men as uniform as the works of nature, the *grammar of language* would be
as indifputable in its principles as the
grammar of nature. But fince good authors have adopted different forms of
fpeech, and in a cafe which admits of no
ftandard but that of *cuftom*, one authority
may be of as much weight as another;
the *analogy of language* is the only thing
to which we can have recourfe, to adjuft
thefe differences. For language, to anfwer the intent of it, which is to exprefs
our

our thoughts with certainty in an inter-
courfe with one another, muft be fixed and
confiftent with itfelf.

By an attention to thefe maxims hath
this grammatical performance been con-
ducted. The beft and the moft numerous
authorities have been carefully followed.
Where they have been contradictory, recourfe hath been had to analogy, as the
laft refource. If this fhould decide for
neither of two contrary practices, the
thing muft remain undecided, till *all-go-
verning cuftom* fhall declare in favour of
the one or the other.

As to a public *Academy*, invefted with
authority to afcertain the ufe of words,
which is a project that fome perfons are
very fanguine in their expectations from, I
think it not only unfuitable to the genius
of a *free nation*, but in itfelf ill calculated
to reform and fix a language. We need
make no doubt but that the beft forms
of fpeech will, in time, eftablifh themfelves by their own fuperior excellence:
and, in all controverfies, it is better to
wait the decifions of *Time*, which are flow
and fure, than to take thofe of *Synods*,
                                    which

which are often hafty and injudicious. A *manufacture* for which there is a great demand, and a *language* which many perfons have leifure to read and write, are both fure to be brought, in time, to all the perfection of which they are capable. What would *Academies* have contributed to the perfection of the *Greek* and *Latin* languages ? Or who, in thofe free ftates, would have fubmitted to them ?

The propriety of introducing the *Englifh grammar* into *Englifh fchools*, cannot be difputed ; a competent knowledge of our own language being both ufeful and ornamental in every profeffion, and a critical knowledge of it abfolutely neceffary to all perfons of a liberal education. The little difficulty there is apprehended to be in the ftudy of it, is the chief reafon, I believe, why it hath been fo much neglected. The *Latin* was fo complex a language that it made, of neceffity (notwithftanding the *Greek* was the learned tongue at Rome) a confiderable branch of Roman fchool education : whereas ours, by being more fimple, is, perhaps, lefs generally underftood. And though the *Grammar-fchool* be, on all accounts, the moft proper place

place for learning it; how many Grammar-fchools have we, and of no fmall reputation, which are deftitute of all provifion for the regular teaching of it? All the fkill that our youth at fchool have in it, being acquired in an indirect manner; *viz.* by the mere practice of ufing it in verbal tranflations.

Indeed, it is not much above a century ago, that our native tongue feemed to be looked upon as below the notice of a claffical fcholar; and men of learning made very little ufe of it, either in converfation, or in writing. And even fince it hath been made the vehicle of knowledge of all kinds, it hath not found its way into the fchools appropriated to language, in proportion to its growing importance; moft of my cotemporaries, I believe, being fenfible, that their knowledge of the grammar of their mother tongue hath been acquired by their own ftudy and obfervation, fince they have paffed the rudiments of the fchools.

To obviate this inconvenience, we muft introduce into our fchools *Englifh grammar*, *Englifh compofitions*, and frequent *Englifh tranf-*

tranflations from authors in other languages. The common objection to Englifh
compofitions, that it is like requiring
brick to be made without ftraw; (boys
not being fuppofed to be capable of fo
much reflection, as is neceffary to treat
any fubject with propriety) is a very fri-
volous one: fince it is very eafy to contrive a variety of exercifes introductory to
Themes upon moral and fcientifical fubjects; in many of which the whole attention may be employed upon language
only; and from thence youth may be
led on in a regular feries of compofitions,
in which the tranfition from *language* to
fentiment may be as gradual and eafy as
poffible.

An Appendix would have been made
to this grammar of examples of *bad Englifh*; for they are really ufeful; but that
they make fo uncouth an appearance in
print. And it can be no manner of trouble to any teacher to fupply the want of
them, by a falfe reading of any good author, and requiring his pupils to point
out, and rectify his miftakes. If any of
the *additional obfervations* be ufed in fchools,
it will be fufficient for the mafter to read
the

the paſſages as he finds them, and to require of his pupils the proper corrections,
and the reaſons alledged for them.

I muſt not conclude this preface, without making my acknowledgements to
Mr. Johnſon, whoſe admirable dictionary
has been of the greateſt uſe to me in the
ſtudy of our language. It is pity he had
not formed as juſt, and as extenſive an
idea of Engliſh grammar. Perhaps this
very uſeful work may ſtill be reſerved for
his diſtinguiſhed abilities in this way.

I muſt, alſo, acknowledge my obliga-
tions to *Dr. Lowth*, whoſe *ſhort introduction to Engliſh grammar* was firſt publiſhed
about a month after the former edition of
mine. Though our plans, definitions of
terms, and opinions, differ very conſider-
ably, I have taken a few of his examples
(though generally for a purpoſe different
from his) to make my own more complete.
He, or any other perſon, is welcome to
make the ſame uſe of thoſe which I have
collected. It is from an amicable union
of labours, together with a generous emulation in all the friends of ſcience, that
we

we may moſt reaſonably expect the exten-
ſion of all kinds of knowledge.

The candid critic will, I hope, ex-
cuſe, and point out to me, any miſtakes
he may think I have fallen into in this performance.   In ſuch a number of obſervations, moſt of them (with reſpect to myſelf, at leaſt) original, it would be very
extraordinary, if none ſhould prove haſty
or injudicious.

THE

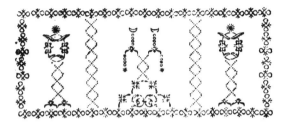

The RUDIMENTS of

ENGLISH GRAMMAR.

The GENERAL DISTRIBUTION.

LANGUAGE is a method of conveying our ideas to the minds of other perfons ; and the *grammar* of any language is a collection of obfervations on the ftructure of it, and a fyftem of rules for the proper ufe of it.

Every language confifts of a number of words, and words confift of letters.

In the Englifh language the following twenty-fix letters are made ufe of; A, a ; B, b ; C, c ; D, d ; E, e ; F, f ; G, g ; H, h ; I, i ; J, j ; K, k ; L, l ; M, m ; N, n ; O, o ; P, p ; Q, q ; R, r ; S, f ; T, t ; U, u ; V, v ; W, w ; X, x ; Y, y ; Z, z.

B   Five

Five of thefe letters, viz. *a, e, i, o, u,* are called *vowels,* and are capable of being diftinctly founded by themfelves. *Y* is alfo fometimes ufed as a vowel, having the fame found as *i.* The conjunction of two vowels makes a *diphthong,* and of three a *triphthong.*

The reft of the letters are called *confonants,* being founded in conjunction with vowels. Of thefe, however, *l, m, n, r, f, s,* are called *femi-vowels,* giving an imperfect found without the help of a vowel ; and *l, m, n, r,* are, moreover, called *liquids.* But *b, c, d, g, k, p, q, t,* are called *mutes,* yielding no found at all without the help of a vowel.

Any number of letters, which together give a diftinct found, make a *fyllable,* and feveral fyllables are generally ufed to compofe a word.

Having given this view of the conftituent parts of the Englifh language, I fhall confider the Grammar of it under the following Heads.

I. Of the inflections of words.

II. Of the grammatical ufe and fignification of certain words; efpecially fuch as the paucity of inflections obliges

obliges us to make ufe of, in order
to exprefs what, in other languages,
is effected by a change of termination, &c.

III. Of Syntax, comprifing the order or
words in a fentence, and the correfpondence of one word to another.

IV. Of Profody, or the rules of verfifi-
cation.

V. Of grammatical figures.

I fhall adopt the ufual diftribution of
words into eight claffes, viz.

NOUNS, ADJECTIVES, PRONOUNS,
VERBS, ADVERBS, PREPOSITIONS,
CONJUNCTIONS, and INTERJECTIONS.

I do this in compliance with the practice of moft *Grammarians*; and becaufe,
if any number, in a thing fo arbitrary,
muft be fixed upon, this feems to be as
comprehenfive and diftinct as any. All
the innovation I have made hath been to
throw out the *Participle*, and fubftitute
the *Adjective*, as more evidently a diftinct
part of fpeech.

B 2   PART

[4]

P A R T I.

Of the Inflections of Words.

S E C T I O N I.
Of the Inflections of Nouns.

Q. WHAT is a Noun?
A. A Noun or (as it is sometimes called) a Substantive, is the name of any thing; as *a Horse, a Tree*; *John, Thomas.*

Q. How many kinds of nouns are there?

A. Two; Proper and Common.

Q. Which are nouns, or substantives, Common?

A. Such as denote the kinds or species of things; as *a Man, a Horse, a River*; which may be understood of any man, any horse, or any river.

Q. Which are called nouns, or substantives, Proper?

A. Such as denote the individuals of any species; as *John, Sarah, the Severn, London.*

Q. What

Q. What changes of termination do nouns admit of ?

A. The terminations of nouns are changed on two accounts principally ; NUMBER, and CASE ; and fometimes alfo on account of GENDER.

Q. How many NUMBERS are there ; and what is meant by NUMBER ?

A. There are two Numbers ; the SINGULAR, when one only is meant ; and the PLURAL, when more are intended.

Q. How is the plural number formed ?

A. The plural number is formed by adding [*s*] to the fingular ; as *River*, *Rivers* ; *Table*, *Tables* : Or [*es*] where [*s*] could not otherwife be founded ; viz. after [*ch*] [*s*] [*sh*] [*x*] and [*z*] as *Fox*, *Foxes* ; *Church*, *Churches*.

Q. What *exceptions* are there to this general rule ?

A. There are two principal exceptions to this rule. 1. The plural of fome nouns ends in [*en*] as *Ox*, *Oxen*. 2. When the fingular ends in [*f*] or [*fe*] the plural ufually ends in [*ves* as *Calf*, *Calves* ; *Wife*, *Wives*. Though there are fome few of thefe terminations that follow the general rule ; as *Muff*, *Muffs* ; *Chief*, *Chiefs*.

Q. Suppofe a noun end in [*y*].

A. In

A. In the plural it is changed into *ies*; as *Fairy, Fairies*; *Gallery, Galleries*.

Q Are there no other irregularities in the formation of numbers, befides thofe that are taken notice of in thefe exceptions?

A. There are feveral plural terminations that can be reduced to no rule; of which are the following, *Die, Dice*; *Goofe, Geefe*; *Foot, Feet*; *Tooth, Teeth*.

Q. Is the plural termination always different from the fingular?

A. No. They are fometimes the very fame; as in the words *Sheep, Deer, &c.*

Q. Have all nouns a fingular termination?

A. No. Some nouns have only a plural termination in ufe; as *Afhes, Bellows, Lungs.*

Q. What are the CASES of nouns?

A. CASES are thofe changes in the terminations of nouns, which ferve to exprefs their relation to other words.

Q. How many cafes are there?

A. There are two cafes; the NOMINATIVE and the GENITIVE.

Q. What is the NOMINATIVE cafe?

A. The NOMINATIVE cafe is that in which we barely name a thing; as *a Man, a Horfe.*

Q. What

Q. What is the GENITIVE cafe?

A. The GENITIVE cafe is that which denotes property or poffeffion; and is formed by adding [s] with an apoftrophe before it to the nominative; as *Solomon's wifdom*; *The Men's wit*; *Venus's· beauty*; or the apoftrophe only in the plural number, when the nominative ends in [s] as the *Stationers' arms.*

Q. Is the relation of property or poffeffion always expreffed by a genitive cafe?

A. No. It is likewife expreffed by the particle [of] before the word; as *the wifdom of Solomon*; *the beauty of Venus*; *the arms of the Stationers.*

Q. How many GENDERS are there? and what is meant by *Gender?*

A. There are two GENDERS; the MASCULINE, to denote the male kind, and the FEMININE, to denote the female.

Q. By what change of termination is the diftinction of gender expreffed?

A. The diftinction of gender (when it is expreffed by a change of termination) is made by adding [efs] to the mafculine to make it feminine; as *Lion, Lionefs*; *Heir, Heirefs.*

8 ENGLISH GRAMMAR.

SECTION II.

Of the Inflections of Adjectives.

Q. WHAT are ADJECTIVES?
A. ADJECTIVES are words that denote the properties or qualities of things; as, *good, tall, swift.*

Q. On what account do adjectives change their terminations?

A. Adjectives change their terminations on account of COMPARISON only.

Q. How many degrees of comparison are there?

A. There are three degrees of comparison; the POSITIVE, in which the quality is barely mentioned; as *hard:* the COMPARATIVE, which expresses the quality somewhat increased, and is formed by adding [r] or [er] to the positive; as *harder*; and the SUPERLATIVE, which expresseth the highest degree of the quality, by adding [ʃ] or [eʃt] to the positive; as *hardeʃt.*

Q. Are all adjectives compared in this manner?

A. No. Some adjectives are compared very irregularly; as the following:

Pof.

Pof.	Comp.	Sup.
Good,	*Better,*	*Beft,*
Bad,	*Worfe,*	*Wcrft,*
Little,	*Lefs,*	*Leaft,*
Much,	*More,*	*Moft.*
Near,	*Nearer,*	*Neareft* or *next.*
Late,	*Later,*	*Lateft* or *laft.*

Q. Are the degrees of comparifon always exprefled by a change of termination?

A. No. Some adjectives, and efpecially *Polyfyllables,* to avoid a harfhnefs in the pronunciation, are compared, not by change of termination, but by particles prefixed; as *benevolent, more bencvolent, moft benevolent.*

Section III.

Of the Inflections of Pronouns.

Q. WHAT are Pronouns?
A. Pronouns are words that
are ufed as fubftitutes for nouns, to prevent the tco frequent and tirefome repetition of them; as *He did this or that*, inftead of exprefsly naming the perfon doing, and the thing done, every time there
is occafion to fpeak of them.

Q. How many kinds of pronouns are
there?

A. There are four kinds of pronouns;
Personal, Possessive, Relative, and
Demonstrative.

Q. Have not fome pronouns a cafe peculiar to themfelves?

A. Yes. It is generally called the Oblique cafe; and is ufed after moft verbs
and prepofitions.

Q. Which are the Personal pronouns?

A. The Personal pronouns are *I*,
thou, *he*, *fhe*, *it*, with their plurals.

Q. How are the perfonal pronouns
formed?

A. Very irregularly, in the following
manner:

Sing.

	Sing.	Plural.
Nominative.	*I.*	*We.*
Oblique cafe.	*Me.*	*Us.*
Nominative.	*Thou.*	*Ye.*
Oblique cafe.	*Thee.*	*You.*
Nominative.	*He. She.*	*They.*
Oblique cafe.	*Him. Her.*	*Them.*
Nominative.	*It.*	*They.*
Oblique cafe.	*It.*	*Them.*
Genitive.	*Its.*	——.

Q. Which are the pronouns POSSES-
SIVE ?

A. The pronouns POSSESSIVE are, *my,
our, thy, your, his, her, their.*

Q. How are the pronouns poffeffive
declined ?

A. Pronouns poffeffive, being wholly
of the nature of adjectives, are, like them,
indeclinable ; except that when they are
ufed without their fubftantives, *my* becomes *mine* ; *thy, thine : our, ours* ; *your,
yours* ; *her, hers* ; *their, theirs* ; as *This
book is mine : This is not yours, but theirs.*

Q. Which are the RELATIVE pronouns ?

A. The RELATIVE pronouns (fo called becaufe they refer, or relate to an antecedent or fubfequent fubftantive) are
who, which, what, and *whether.*

Q. How is *who* declined ?

A.   Sing. and plural.

Nominative. *Who.*

Genitive.   *Whoſe.*

Oblique.   *Whom.*

Q. Are *which, what,* and *whether,* de-clinable ?

A. No.   Except *whoſe* may be ſaid to be the genitive of *which.*

Q. What is meant by the ANTECE-DENT of a relative ?

A. That preceding noun to which it is related, as an adjective is to its ſub-ſtantive ; as the word *Darius,* when we ſay, *This is Darius whom Alexander con-quered.*

Q. Which are the pronouns DEMON-STRATIVE.

A. The pronouns DEMONSTRATIVE are *this, that, other,* and *the ſame.*

Q. How are the demonſtrative pro-nouns declined ?

A. *This* makes *theſe,* and *that* makes *thoſe* in the plural number ; and *other* makes *others* when it is found without it's ſubſtantive.

SECTION

VERBS.   13

SECTION IV.

Of the Inflections of Verbs.

Q. WHAT is a VERB?
A.   A VERB is a word that expresseth what is affirmed of, or attributed
to a thing; as *I love*; *the horse neighs.*
 Q. What is meant by the SUBJECT of
an affirmation?
 A. The perfon or thing concerning
which the affirmation is made. When
we fay *Alexander conquered Darius*, Alexander is the fubject; becaufe we affirm
concerning him, that he conquered Darius.
 Q. How many kinds of verbs are
there?
 A. Two; TRANSITIVE and NEUTER.
 Q. What is a verb tranfitive?
 A. A verb tranfitive, befides having a
fubject, implies, likewife, an object of the
affirmation, upon which its meaning may,
as it were, pafs; and without which the
fenfe would not be complete. The verb
to conquer is tranfitive, becaufe it implies
an object, that is, a perfon or kingdom,
&c. conquered; and *Darius* is that object,
when we fay, *Alexander conquered Darius.*
                                        Q. What

Q. What is a verb NEUTER ?

A. A verb neuter has no object, different from the subject of the affirmation; as *to rest*. When we say *Alexander resteth*, the sense is complete, without any other words.

Q. What is the RADICAL FORM of verbs, or that from which all other forms and modifications of them are derived ?

A. The RADICAL FORM of verbs is that in which they follow the particle *to*; as *to love*.

Q. What circumstances affect the terminations of verbs ?

A. Two. TENSE and PERSON; besides NUMBER, which they have in common with nouns.

Q. How many TENSES have verbs ?

A. Verbs have two TENSES; the PRESENT TENSE, denoting the *time present*; and the PRETER TENSE, which expresseth the *time past*.

Q. What changes of termination do these *tenses* of verbs occasion.

A. The first person of the preter tense is generally formed by adding [*ed*] or [*d*] to the first person of the present tense (which is the same as the radical form of the verb) as *I love, I loved.* But many verbs form their preter tense without regard
gard

gard to any rule or analogy; as *to awake,
I awoke ; to think, I thought.*

Q. What changes of termination are occafioned by the *perfons* of verbs ?

A. In both tenfes, the fecond perfon fingular adds [*ft*] or [*eft*] to the firft perfon (which, in the third perfon fingular of the prefent tenfe, changes into [*eth*] or [*es*]) all the perfons of the plural number retaining the termination of the firft perfon fingular.

Q. Give an example of a verb formed in its tenfes and perfons.

A.   Prefent Tenfe.

Singular.	Plural.
I love.	*We love.*
Thou lovest.	*Ye love.*
He loveth, or *loves.*	*They love.*

Preter Tenfe.

I loved.	*We loved.*
Thou lovedft.	*Ye loved.*
He loved.	*They loved.*

Prefent Tenfe.

I grant.	*We grant.*
Thou grantest.	*Ye grant.*
He granteth or *grants.*	*They grant.*

Preter

Preter Tenfe.

Singular.	Plural.
I granted.	*We granted.*
Thou grantedft.	*Ye granted.*
He granted.	*They granted.*

Q. Are thefe changes of termination in the perfons of verbs always obferved?

A. No. They are generally omitted after the words, *if, though, e'er, before, whether, except, whatfoever, whomfoever,* and words of *wifhing*: as *Doubtlefs thou art our father, though Abraham* acknowledge *us not*; [not *acknowledgeth*].

Q. What is this form of the tenfes called?

A. This form, becaufe it is rarely ufed but in conjunction with fome or other of the preceding words, may be called the *conjunctive* form of the tenfes. It is as follows.

Conjunctive Prefent.

Singular.	Plural.
If I love.	*If we love.*
If thou love.	*If ye love.*
If he love.	*If they love.*

Conjunctive Preter Tenfe.

If I loved.	*If we loved.*
If thou loved.	*If ye loved.*
If he loved.	*If they loved.*

Q. What

Q. What are the PARTICIPLES of verbs?

A. PARTICIPLES are adjectives derived from verbs, and retaining their signification.

Q. How many participles hath a verb?

A. A verb hath two participles. 1. The participle *Present*, which denotes that the action spoken of is then taking place, and ends in [*ing*] as *hearing*, *writing*. 2. The participle *Pret rite*, which denotes its being past, and ends in [*ed*] being the same with the first person of the preter tense; as *loved*.

Q. Do all participles preterite end in [*ed*]?

A. No. There are many participles preterite, which neither end in [*ed*] nor take any other termination of the preter tense; as to *begin*, Preter, *I began*. Part. It is *begun*. To *die*, Preter, He *died*. Part. He is *dead*: moreover, some verbs have two participles preterite, which may be used indifferently; as to *load*; he is *loaded*; he is *laden*. To *sow*; it is *sowed*; it is *sown*.

Q. In what sense is a verb to be understood, when it occurs in its radical form?

A. It hath, then, the force of a command from the person speaking to the
person

person or persons to whom it is addressed; as, *write*, i. e. *do thou*, or *do ye write*.

Q. What is the meaning of the RA- DICAL FORM of a verb preceded by the particle *to* ?

A. It is then no more than the name of an action or state ; as, *to die* is common to all men; i. e. *death* is common to all men.

Q. What are AUXILIARY verbs ?

A. AUXILIARY verbs are verbs that are used in conjunction with other verbs, to ascertain the time, and other circum- stances of an action with greater exact- nefs.

Q. Which are the principal auxiliary verbs ?

A. The principal auxiliary verbs are *to do*, *to have*, *to be*, and the imperfect verbs *shall*, *will*, *can*, *may*, and *must*.

Q. How are these verbs inflected ?

A. They are all inflected with confi- derable irregularity ; and the verbs *shall*, *will*, *can*, and *may*, express no certain dif- tinction of time ; and, therefore, have no proper tenses : but they have two forms, one of which expresses absolute certainty, and may, therefore, be called the *abfo- lute form*; and the other implies a con- dition, and may, therefore, be called the *conditional form*. Q. What

Q. What are the inflections of the verbs *to do*, *to have*, and *to be*.

To *Do*.

Prefent Tenfe.

Sing.	Plural.
I do.	*We do.*
Thou doeft, or *doft*.	*Ye do.*
He doth, or *does*.	*They do.*

(a) Preter Tenfe.

I did.	*We did.*
Thou didft.	*Ye did.*
He did.	*They did.*

Participles.

Prefent. *Doing*.
Preterite. *Done*.

To *Have*.

Prefent Tenfe.

I have.	*We have.*
Thou haft.	*Ye have.*
He hath, or *has*.	*They have.*

(a) After each tenfe may be fubjoined the *conjunctive form* of it; as, *If I do, if thou do. If I did, if thou did*, &c.

Preter Tenſe.

Sing.	Plural.
I had.	*We had.*
Thou hadſt.	*Ye had.*
He had.	*They had.*

Participles.

Preſent. *Havng.*

Preter. *Had.*

To *Be*.

Preſent Tenſe.

I am.	*We are.*
Thou art.	*Ye are.*
He is.	*They are.*

Conjunctive form of the preſent tenſe.

If I be.	*If we be.*
If thou be (b).	*If ye be.*
If he be.	*If they be.*

Preter Tenſe.

I was.	*We were.*
Thou waſt.	*Ye were.*
He was.	*They were.*

Conjunctive Form.

If I were.	*If we were.*
If thou wert.	*If ye were.*
If he were.	*If they were.*

(b) Mr. *Johnſon* ſays *beeſt.*

Parti-

VERBS.

Participles.

Prefent. *Being.*

Preter. *Been.*

Q. What are the inflections of the verbs *fhall, will, may, can,* and *muft?*

A. *Shall.*

ABSOLUTE Form.

Sing.	Plural.
I *fhall.*	We *fhall.*
Thou *fhalt.*	Ye *fhall.*
He *fhall.*	They *fhall.*

CONDITIONAL Form.

I *fhould.*	We *fhould.*
Thou *fhouldeft.*	Ye *fhould*
He *fhould.*	They *fhould.*

Will.

ABSOLUTE Form.

I *will.*	We *will.*
Thou *wilt.*	Ye *will.*
He *will.*	They *wil.*

CONDITIONAL Form.

I *would.*	We *would.*
Thou *wouldeft.*	Ye *would.*
He *would.*	They *would.*

May.

May.

Absolúte Form.

Sing.	Plural.
I may.	*We may.*
Thou mayeſt.	*Ye may.*
He may.	*They may.*

Conditional Form.

I might.	*We might.*
Thou mighteſt.	*Ye might.*
He might.	*They might.*

Can.

Absolute Form.

I can.	*We can.*
Thou canſt.	*Ye can.*
He can.	*They can.*

Conditional Form.

I could.	*We could.*
Thou couldeſt.	*Ye could.*
He could.	*They could.*

Muſt.

Preſent Tenſe.

I muſt.	*We muſt.*
Thou muſt.	*Ye muſt.*
He muſt.	*They muſt.*

Q. What

VERBS.

VERBS. 23

Q. What are the COMPOUND TENSES of verbs?

A. The COMPOUND TENSES of verbs are the tenſes of auxiliary verbs uſed in conjunction with ſome form, or participle of other verbs ; as *I ſhall hear, I may have heard.*

Q. In what manner are the auxiliary verbs uſed in conjunction with other verbs ?

A. To the ſeveral tenſes of the auxiliary verb *to have*, is joined the *participle preterite*, as *I have written, I have been.* To thoſe of the verb *to be*, are joined both the participles ; the *preſent* and *preterite:* as *I am hearing*, and *I am heard* ; and to all the reſt of the auxiliary verbs is joined the *radical form* of the verb ; as *I ſhall, will, may, muſt, can*, or *do write* ; *I ſhall, will, may, muſt*, or *can be.*

Q. Into how many *claſſes*, or *orders*, may the compound tenſes of verbs be diſtributed ?

A. The compound tenſes of verbs may be commodiouſly diſtributed into three diſtinct claſſes or orders ; according as the auxiliary verbs that conſtitute them require the *radical form*, the *participle preſent*, or the *participle preterite* to be joined with them. They are likewiſe

ſingle,

single, double, or *triple,* according as *one,
two,* or *three* auxiliary verbs are made
uſe of.

Q. Repeat the compound tenſes of the
verb *to hear.*

A. The compound tenſes of the *firſt
order,* or thoſe in which the *radical form*
of the principal verb is made uſe of.

> *Will, can, may, muſt,* or *ſhall hear.*

Abſolute ⎱ *I ſhall hear, Thou ſhalt hear,*
form. ⎰   *He ſhall hear,* &c.
Conditi- ⎱ *I ſhould hear, Thou ſhouldſt*
onal. ⎰   *hear, He ſhould hear,* &c. (d)

The compound tenſes of the *ſecond order,* or thoſe in which the participle preſent
is made uſe of.

> *To be hearing.*

Preſent ⎱ *I am hearing, Thou art*
tenſe. ⎰   *hearing,* &c.
Conjunct- ⎱ *If I be hearing, If thou be*
ive form. ⎰   *hearing,* &c.
Preterite. }   *I was hearing, Thou waſt
hearing,* &c.

(d) In the ſame manner form the tenſes made by
will, can, may, and *muſt.* The conjunctive form
of the tenſes may likewiſe be ſupplied in its proper
place, if it be thought neceſſary.

†

Con-

Conjunct- } *If I were hearing, If thou*
ive.   } *wert hearing,* &c.

Participle prefent. *Being hearing.*
Participle preterite. *Been hearing.*

The firſt Double Compound.

Shall be hearing.

Abſolute   } *I ſhall be hearing, Thou ſhalt*
form.   } *be hearing,* &c.
Conditi-   } *I ſhould be hearing, Thou*
onal.   } *ſhouldeſt be hearing,* &c.

The ſecond Double Compound.

To have been hearing.

Preſent   } *I have been hearing, Thou haſt*
tenſe.   } *been hearing,* &c.
Preterite. } *I had been hearing, Thou hadſt*
           } *been hearing,* &c.
Participle prefent. *Having been hearing.*

The Triple Compound.

Shall have been hearing.

Abſolute   } *I ſhall have been hearing, Thou*
form.   } *ſhalt have,* &c.
Conditi-   } *I ſhould have been hearing,*
onal.   } *Thou ſhouldeſt have,* &c.

C   The

The compound tenfes of the *third order*; viz. thofe in which the participle preterite of the principal verb is ufed.

To be heard.

Prefent tenfe.	*I am heard, Thou art heard,* &c.
Conjunct-ive form.	*If I be heard, If thou be heard,* &c.
Preterite.	*I was heard, Thou waft heard,* &c.
Conjunct-ive.	*If I were heard, if thou wert heard,* &c.

Participle prefent. *Being heard.*
—— preterite. *Been heard.*

The firft Double Compound.

Shall be heard.

Abfolute form.	*I fhall be heard, Thou fhalt be heard,* &c.
Conditi-onal.	*I fhould be heard, Thou fhould-eft,* &c.

The fecond Double Compound.

Shall have heard.

Abfolute form.	*I fhall have heard, Thou fhalt have,* &c.
Conditi-onal.	*I fhould have heard, Thou fhouldeft,* &c.

The

The third Double Compound.

To have been heard.

Prefent } *I have been heard, Thou haft*
tenfe. } *been heard,* &c.

Preterite. } *I had been heard, Thou hadft*
} *been heard,* &c.

Participle prefent. *Having been heard.*

The Triple Compound.

Shall have been heard.

Abfolute } *I fhall have been heard, Thou,*
form. } &c.

Conditi- } *I fhould have been heard, Thou*
onal. } *fhouldeft,* &c.

Q. What do you obferve concerning thefe compound tenfes?

A. It is obfervable that, in forming the tenfes, all the change of termination is confined to the auxiliary that is named firft ; and therefore, fecondly, That if the auxiliary which is firft named, have no participle, there is no participle belonging to the tenfes that are made by it.

To this fection concerning the inflections of words, it may be convenient to fubjoin an account of thofe claffes which admit of few, or no inflections.

Q. What

Q. What are ADVERBS?

A. ADVERBS are contractions of sentences, or of clauses of a sentence, generally serving to denote the *manner*, and other *circumstances* of an action; as *wisely*, i. e. in a wise manner; *now*, i. e. at this time; *here*, in this place.

Q. How many kinds of adverbs are there?

A. Adverbs may be distributed into as many kinds as there are circumstances of an action. They may, therefore, be referred to a great variety of heads. The principal of them are the three following; *viz.* 1st, Those of *Place*; as *here*, *there*. 2dly, Those of *Time*; as *often*, *sometimes*, *presently*. And, 3dly, Those of *Quality or Manner*, which are derived from adjectives by adding [*ly*] to them; as, *wisely*, *happily*, *firstly*; from *wise*, *happy*, *first*.

Q. What is a PREPOSITION?

A. A PREPOSITION is a word that expresseth the relation that one word hath to another; such as *of*, *with*, *from*, *to*: as, *He bought it* with *money, He went* to *London*.

Q. What are CONJUNCTIONS?

A. CONJUNCTIONS are words that join sentences together, and shew the manner

of

of their dependence upon one another; as *and*, *if*, *but*, &c.

Q. What are INTERJECTIONS?

A. INTERJECTIONS are broken or imperfect words, denoting some emotion or passion of the mind; as, *ah*, *oh*, *phy*.

It may not be improper, also, to lay down, in this place, for the use of learners, *Easy rules to distinguish the several parts of speech.*

A *Substantive* admits of [*a*] [*the*] *good*, *bad*, or some other known adjective before it; as, a good *man*.

An *Adjective* hath no determinate meaning with only [*a*] or [*the*] before it; but requires *man* or *thing* after it; and admits of degrees of comparison; as a *good* man, a *better* man.

A *Verb* admits of the personal pronouns before it, as *He loves*, *They love*.

Pronouns have been enumerated.

Adverbs do all, or most of them, answer to some one of these questions, *How? How much? When?* or *Where?* when the answer gives no word that is known, by the preceding rules, to be a substantive or adjective.

Prepositions easily admit the oblique cases of the personal pronouns, *me*, *him*,

C 3   *her*,

30   ENGLISH GRAMMAR.

ber, &c. to follow them ; as *to me, with me, among them.*

Conjunctions and *Interjections* are eafily known by their definitions.

Section V.
Of the Derivation and Compofition of Words.

BEfides the conftant and regular in-flections of words, of which an ac-count has been given in the preceding fections ; there are many other changes, by means of which words pafs from one clafs to another : but, becaufe only fome of the words of any clafs admit of a fi-milar change, they are not ufually enu-merated among the grammatical changes of terminations. In nothing, however, is the genius of a language more apparent than in fuch changes ; and, were they uniform and conftant, they would have the fame right to be taken notice of by grammarians that any other inflections have.   Of thefe changes I fhall here give the following fhort fummary, extracted chiefly from Mr. Johnfon.

Nouns

Nouns are frequently converted into *verbs* by lengthening the found of their vowels; as *to houfe, to braze, to glaze, to breathe*; from *houfe, brafs, glafs, breath.*

Sometimes nouns are elegantly converted into verbs without any change at all. *Cufhioned,* Bolingbroke. *Diademed,* Pope. *Ribboned,* Lady M. W. Montague.

Verbs, with little or no variation, are converted into *fubftantives,* expreffing what is denoted by the verb as done or procured; as *love,* a *fright*; from *to love, to fright*; and a *ftroke,* from *ftruck,* the preterite of the verb *to ftrike.*

Befides thefe, words of the following terminations are generally derivative; *nouns* ending in

—*er,* derived from *verbs,* fignify the agent; as *lover, writer, ftriker.*

Some nouns of this clafs, in confequence of frequent ufe, have ceafed to be confidered as belonging to it; and in this cafe the *e* is often changed into fome other vowel, as *liar, conductor.*

—*ing,* fignify the *action* of the verb they are derived from; as *the frighting, the ftriking.*

—*th,* are *abftract fubftantives* derived from *concrete adjectives*; as *length, ftrength, dearth*; from *long, ftrong, dear.*

C 4   —*nefs,*

—*nefs,* ⎫ denote *charaƐer* or *quality* ; as
—*hood,* or ⎬   *whitenefs; hardnefs, manhood,*
—*head,* ⎭   *widowhood, godhead.*

—*fhip,* fignify *office, employment, ftate,* or
    condition ; as *kingfhip, ftewardfhip.*

—*ery,* aƐion or habit ; as *knavery, fool-*
    ery, roguery.

—*wick,* ⎫
—*rick,* ⎬ jurifdiƐion ; as, *bailiwick, bifhop-*
—*ry,* ⎬   *rick, deanry, kingdom.*
—*aom,* ⎭

—*ian,* profeffion ; as, *theologian, phyfician.*

—*ard,* charaƐer or habit ; as, *drunkard,*
    dotard, dullara.

            ⎫ are derived from the French,
—*ment* and ⎬   and generally fignify the
—*age,*   ⎬   *aƐ* or the *habit* ; as com-
          ⎭   *mandment, ufage.*

—*eé,* the poffeffor (of French original alfo)
    as, *granteé,* one to whom a grant is
    made ; *leffeé,* to whom the leafe is
    made, *&c.*

Nouns fometimes become *diminutives* by
the addition of [*in*] or fome other pro-
duƐion of their termination ; as *goflin,
lambkin, hillock, pickerel, rivulet.*

AdjeƐives ending in

         ⎰ are generally derived from *nouns,*
—*y* and ⎨   and fignify *plenty* and *abundance* ;
         ⎱ as *loufy, airy, joyful, fruitful.*

                             —*fome*

—some (q. d. *something*; i. e. in *some degree*) fignify likewife-*plenty*, but in a lefs degree than the terminations [*y*] and [*ful*] as *gamefome, lonefome.*

—lefs, fignify *want,* as *worthlefs, joylefs.*

—ly, (q. d. *like*) fignify *likenefs* ; as *giantly, heavenly.*

—ifh, fignify *fimilitude* or tendency to a character; as *whitifh, thievifh, childifh*; alfo belonging to a nation; as *Danifh, Spanifh, Irifh.*

—able, derived from nouns or verbs, fignify *capacity* ; as *comfortable, tenable, improveable.*

Verbs ending in

—en, are frequently derived from adjectives, and fignify the production of the quality ; as *to lengthen, to ftrengthen.*

The participles prefixed to words, with their ufe in compofition, are the following :

Ante—fignifies *before* ; as *Antediluvian.*

Anti—and ⎱ *againft* ; as *Antimonarchical,*

Contra— ⎰ *contradict.*

Circum—*about*; as *circumfcribe.*

De—*down* ; as *depofe, depreciate.*

Dis—negation, or privation; as *difbelieve. diflike, difarm.*

C 5 *In*

In (changed fometimes into [*im*] before [*m*] into [*il*] always before [*l*] into [*ir*] before [*r*] in words derived from the Latin, and into [*un*] in other words) fignifies negation; as *unpleafant, ineffectual, imperfect, illegitimate, irrefragable.*

Mifs—*error*; as *miftake, mifreprefent.*

Per—*through*; as *perfuade, perfift.*

Poft—*after*; as *poftpone.*

Preter—*beyond* (in power) as *preternatural.*

Ultra—*beyond* (in place) as *Ultramontane.*

Inter —*among*; as *intermix.*

Tranf—*over*; as *transfer, tranflate.*

Re—*again*, or *backward*; as *revolve, r bound.*

Super—*above*; as *fupernatural.*

Sub—*under*; as *fubfcribe.*

P A R T

PART II.

Of the grammatical Use and Signification of certain Words, especially such as the paucity of our inflections obliges us to make use of, in order to express what, in other languages, is effected by a change of termination.

SECTION I.

Of the Articles.

Q. WHAT are ARTICLES?

A. Articles are the words [*a*] and [*the*] placed before nouns, to ascertain the extent of their signification.

Q. What is the use of the article [*a*]?

A. The article [*a*] (before a consonant, but [*an*] before a vowel) intimates that one only of a species is meant, but not any one in particular; as, *This is a good book*; *i. e.* One among the books that are good. Hence it is called the article *Indefinite*.

C 6   Q. What

Q. What is the use of the article [*the*]?

A. The article [*the*] limits the signifi-cation of a word to one or more of a species ; as *This is the book* ; *These are the men* ; *i. e.* this particular book, and these particular men. For this reason it is called the article *Definite*.

Q. In what sense is a noun to be under-stood, when neither of these articles is prefixed to it ?

A. Generally, in an unlimited sense, expressing not one in general, or one in particular, but every individual that can be comprehended in the term, as, *Man* is born to trouble ; i. e. whoever par-takes of human nature, *all mankind*.

SECTION II.

Of the Ufe of the Auxiliary Verbs.

Q. IN what manner doth the auxiliary
verb *to do* affect the fignification
of verbs.

A. It only renders the affirmation the
more *emphatical*; as *I do love, I did hate*;
i. e. *I love indeed, Indeed I hated.*

Q. In what manner doth the auxiliary
verb *to be* affect the fignification of verbs?

A. The auxiliary verb *to be,* joined with
the *participle prefent* of a verb, expreffes
the affirmation with the greater emphafis
and precifion; as *I am writing,* i. e. *in the
very action of writing*; and joined to the
participle preterite of a verb, it fignifies
the fuffering or receiving the action expreffed; as *I am loved, I was hated.*

Q. What is the ufe of the auxiliary
verbs *fhall* and *will.*

A. When we fimply *foretel,* we ufe
fhall in the firft perfon, and *will* in the reft;
as *I fhall,* or *he will write:* but when we
promife, threaten, or *engage,* we ufe *will* in
the firft perfon, and *fhall* in the reft; as
I will, or *he fhall write.*

Q. In what manner do the auxiliary
verbs

verbs *can*, *may*, and *muſt*, affect the fig
nification of verbs?

A. In the *abſolute form*, the auxiliary
verb *can*, ſignifies a preſent *power*; *may*,
a *right*; and *muſt*, a *neceſſity* to do ſomething that is not yet done; as *I can, may*
or *muſt, write*; and the *conditional forms could*
and *might*, ſignify likewiſe, a *power* and
right to do what is affirmed, but imply the
intervention of ſome obſtacle or impedi-
ment, that prevents its taking place; as *I
could*, or *might write*; i. e. if nothing hin-
dered.—The like may alſo be obſerved of.
the *conditional forms* of *ſhall* and *will*.

Q. In what manner doth the auxiliary
verb *to have* affect the ſignification of
verbs?

A. The auxiliary verb *to have* ſignifies.
that what is affirmed is or was paſt; as *I
have received, I had written*; i. e. the action of receiving is now paſt, and the action of writing was then over.

Q. In what manner doth the auxiliary.
verb *to have* determine the time of any
action?

A. When we make uſe of the auxiliary
verb *to have*, we have no idea of any certain portion of time intervening between
the time of the action and the time of
ſpeaking of it; the time of the action
being

being fome period that extends to the prefent ; as, *I have this year*, or *this morning, written*; fpoken in the fame year, or the fame morning : whereas, fpeaking of any action done in a period of time that is wholly expired, we ufe the preter tenfe of the verb ; as *laft year*, or *yefterday, I wrote a letter* : intimating, that fome certain portion of time is paft between the time of the action, and the time of fpeaking of it.

Q. Are there no other verbs, befides thofe which are called *auxiliary*, that are joined in conftruction with other verbs, without being followed by the prepofition *to* ?

A. The verbs *bid, dare, read, make, fee, hear, feel*, and alfo *act*, are ufed in the fame conftruction; as, *He faw me write it. I heard him fay it.*

One of the greateft difficulties in the Englifh language, relates to t e fubject of this part; as it confifts in the ufe of the conjunctive particles and prepofitions particularly *of, to, for, with*, and *in*, with a few others. Indeed, there is nothing in which the practice of our beft authors is more variable or capricious : but I thought it would be beft, to throw all the remarks

remarks I have made on this fubject, into the *Additional Obfervations.*

****

P A R T III.

*Of Syntax; comprifing the Order of
Words in a fentence, and the Correfpondence of one Word to another.*

Q. WHAT is the ufual place for
the fubject of the affirmation,
in an affirmative fentence?

A. Before the verb; as the word *Alexander* in the fentence, *Alexander conquered
Darius.*

Q. What is its place in an interroga-
tive fentence?

A. Between the auxiliary and the radical form of the principal verb; as, *Did
Alexander conquer Darius?*

Q. What is the ufual place for the object of an affirmation?

A. After the verb, as the word *Darius*
in the fentence, *Alexander conquered Darius.*

Q. What is the ufual place of the adjective?

A. Im-

A. Immediately before the fubftantive; as, *a good man, a fine horfe.*

Q. In what cafes is the adjective placed after the fubftantive?

A. When a claufe of a fentence depends upon the adjective; as, *a* man generous *to his enemies. Feed me with* food convenient *for me.*

Q What is the proper place for the pronoun relative?

A. Immediately after its antecedent; as, *That is the* Darius, whom *Alexander conquered.*

Q. What is the moft convenient place for an adverb, or a feparate claufe of a fentence?

A. Between the fubject and the verb; as, *Alexander* intirely *conquered Darius. Alexander, in three battles, conquered Darius.* Or between the auxiliaries and the verb or participle; as, *You have prefently difpatched this bufinefs. I have been exceedingly pleafed.*

Q. What is the correfpondence of the adjective pronouns with their fubftantives?

A. They muft agree in number; as, *This man. Thefe men.*

Q. What is the correfpondence of the verb and its fubject?

A. They

A. They muſt have the ſame number and perſon ; as, *I love. Thou loveſt. He loves. The ſun ſhines, &c.*

Q. Suppoſe there be two ſubjects of the ſame affirmation, and they be both of the ſingular number?

A. The verb correſponding to them muſt be in the plural ; as, *Your* youth *and* merit have *been abuſed.*

Q. In what circumſtances is the oblique caſe of pronouns uſed ?

A. After verbs tranſitive and prepoſitions ; as, *He loves* her. *I gave the book to* him.

As but few of the relations of words and ſentences in conſtruction are expreſſed by a change of termination in Engliſh, but generally by conjunctive particles, the art of Engliſh Syntax muſt conſiſt, chiefly, in the proper application of the *conjunctive particles* ; and the accurate uſe of theſe can only be learned from *obſervation* and a *dictionary.*

What I have obſerved on this ſubject will be found among the *Additional Obſervations.*

P A R T

PART IV.

Of Prosody.

Q. WHAT is Prosody?

A. Prosody is that part of Grammar which teaches the rules of *Pronunciation*, and of *Versification*.

Q. Wherein consists. the art of *Pronunciation?*

A. In laying the *accent* upon the proper syllable of a word, and the *emphasis* upon the proper word of a sentence.

Q. Upon what doth the art of *Versification* depend.

A. Upon arranging the syllables of words according to certain laws, respecting *quantity* or *accent*.

Q. What is most observable in the arrangement of. syllables according to their quantity?

A. If the accent fall upon the *first* syllable, the *third*, the *fifth*, &c. the verse is said to consist of *Trochees*; which is called a foot of two syllables, whereof the first is long, and the second short.

If it fall upon the *second*, the *fourth*, the *sixth*, &c. as is most usual in English verse,

it

it is faid to confift of *Iambics*; which are feet of two fyllables, whereof the firft is fhort, and the fecond long. If two fyllables be pronounced both long, the foot is called a *fpondee*; and if one long fyllable be fucceeded by two fhort ones continually, the verfe is faid to confift of *Dactyls*. I fhall give a fhort fpecimen of each of thefe kinds of verfe.

Trochaical.
In thĕ | dāys ŏf | ōld,
Stōrĭes | plainly | tōld,

(e) *Iambic.*
Wīth rā | vĭfh'd eārs
Thĕ mōn | ărch heārs.

Dactylic, fometimes called *Anapæftic.*
Dĭ | ōgĕnĕs | fūrlў ănd | prōud.

Verfes confift of more or fewer of thefe feet at pleafure; and verfes of different lengths intermixed form a *Pindarick* poem.

(e) A *Spondee*, with which Iambic verfes abound.

Part V.

Of Figures.

FIGURES are thofe deviations from grammatical or natural propriety, which are either allowed or admired.

Thofe which affect Englifh *letters* or *fyllables*, and which may therefore be termed *Orthographical* figures, are *Aphære-fis*, when a fyllable or letter is omitted at the beginning of a word; as *'tis*, for *it is*; *Syncope*, when it is left out in the middle; as *ne er* for *never*; and *Apocope*, when omitted at the end; as *tho'* for *though*.

The omiffion of a word neceffary to grammatical propriety, is called *Ellipfis*; as *I wifh you would write*, for *I wifh that you would write*.

Particles, and fome other words, muft frequently be fupplied to make the conftruction complete; as in the following fentences. *I value it not a* (or *of a*) *farthing*; i. e. *at the price of a farthing*: *at twelve o' clock*; i. e. *of the clock*.

The

The pronoun relative is frequently o-mitted; as, *The houfe I have built*; inftead of faying, *The houfe that*, or *which*, *I have built*. To make very frequent ufe of this ellipfis feems to be a fault.

With refpect to the *ufe of figures* it is obferved, that the *orthographical figures* are not ufed with approbation, except in very *familiar writing*, or *verfe*.

A N

A N

APPENDIX,

Containing a Catalogue of Verbs irregularly inflected.

THAT I might not crowd the notes too much, I have chofen to throw into an Appendix, *a catalogue of verbs irregularly inflected*, excluding thofe verbs, and parts of verbs, which are become obfolete; that learners may be at no lofs what form of expreffion to prefer. It is extracted chiefly from Mr. *Ward*'s catalogue; but without taking any notice of his diftinction of conjugations. When the regular inflection is in ufe, as well as the irregular one, an afterifm is put.

Radical form.	*Preter tenfe.*	*Participle pret.*
arife.	arofe.	arifen.
awake.	awoke.*	awoke.*
bear, or *bring forth.*	} bare.	born.
bear, or *carry.*	bore.	borne.

beat.

Radical form.	*Preter tenfe.*	*Participle pret.*
beat.	beat.	beaten.
begin.	began.	begun.
bereave.	bereft.*	bereft.*
befeech.	befought.	befought.*
bid.	bade.	bidden.
bind.	bound.	bound.
bite.	bit.	bitten.
blow.	blew.	blown.
bleed.	bled.	bled.
break.	brake.	broken, broke
breed.	bred.	bred.
bring.	brought.	brought.
burft.	burft.	burft, burften.
buy.	bought.	bought.
caft.	caft.	caft.
catch.	caught.*	caught.*
chide.	chid.	chidden.
chufe.	chofe.	chofen.
cleave.	clave.	cloven, cleft
cling.	clung.	clung.
clothe.	clad.*	clad.*
come.	came.	come.
coft.	coft.	coft.
crew.	crew.	crowed.
cut.	cut.	cut.
dare.	durft.*	dared.
die.	died.	dead.
dig.	dug.*	dug.*
draw.	drew.	drawn.

†   drink.

Radical form.	Preter tense.	Participle pret.
drink.	drank.	drunk.
drive.	drove.	driven.
eat.	ate.	eaten.
fall.	fell.	fallen.
feed.	fed.	fed.
fight.	fought.	fought.
find.	found.	found.
flee.	fled.	fled.
fling.	flung.	flung.
fly.	flew.	flown.
forsake.	forsook.	forsaken.
freeze.	froze.	frozen.
get.	gat, got.	gotten.
give.	gave.	given.
go	went.	gone.
grind.	ground.	ground.
grow.	grew.	grown.
hang.	hung.*	hung.
hew.	hewed.	hewn.
hide.	hid.	hidden.
hit.	hit.	hit.
hold.	held.	holden, ·held
hurt.	hurt.	hurt.
keep.	kept.	kept.
knit.	knitted.	knitted, knit.
know.	knew	known.
lay.	laid.	laid, lain.
lead.	led.	led.

D

leave.

Radical form.	Preter tenſe.	Participle pret.
leave.	left.	left.
let.	let.	let.
lie.	lay.	lain.
load.	loaded.	loaden, laden*
loſe.	loſt.	loſt.
make.	made.	made.
meet.	met.	met.
mow.	mowed.	mown.*
pay.	paid.	paid.
put.	put.	put.
———	quoth he.	———
read.	read.	read.
rend.	rent.	rent.
ring.	rung, rang.	rung.
rive.	rived.	riven.
riſe.	roſe.	riſen.
ride.	rode.	ridden.
run.	ran	run.
ſaw.	ſawed.	ſawn.
ſee.	ſaw.	ſeen.
ſeek.	ſought.	ſought.
ſeethe.	ſeethed.	ſodden.
ſell.	ſold.	ſold.
ſend.	ſent.	ſent.
ſet.	ſet.	ſet.
ſhake.	ſhook.	ſhaken.
ſhave.	ſhaved.	ſhaven.*
ſhear.	ſheared.	ſhorn.

ſhed.

Radical form.	Preter tense.	Participle pret.
shed.	shed.	shed.
shine.	shone.	shone.*
shoe.	shod.	shod.
shoot	shot.	shot.
show, shew.	showed, shewed.	shown,* shewn.*
shrink.	shrank, shrunk	shrunk.
shut.	shut.	shut.
sing.	sang.	sung.
sink.	sunk.	sunk.
sit.	sat.	sat.
slay.	slew.	slain.
slide.	slided.	slidden.
slink.	slunk.	slunk.
sling.	slung.	slung.
slit.	slit.	slit.
smite.	smote.	smitten.
sow.	sowed.	sown.*
speak.	spoke.	spoken.
speed.	sped.	sped.
spend.	spent.	spent.
spin.	spun.	spun.
spit.	spat.	spitted.
split.	split.	split.
spread.	spread.	spread.
spring.	sprung, sprang	sprung.
stand.	stood.	stood.
steal.	stole.	stolen.
stick.	stuck.	stuck.

sting.

Radical form.	Preter tense.	Participle pret.
sting.	stung.	stung.
stink.	stank.	stunk.
stride.	strode.	stridden
strike.	struck.	stricken.
string.	strung.	strung.
strive.	strove.	striven.
strow.	strowed.	strown.
swear.	swore, sware.	sworn.
sweat.	sweat.	sweat.
swell.	swelled.	swollen.*
swim.	swam.	swum.
swing.	swung.	swung.
take.	took.	taken.
teach.	taught.	taught.
tear.	tore, tare.	torn.
tell.	told.	told.
think.	thought.	thought.
thrive.	throve.	thriven.
throw.	threw.	thrown.
thrust.	thrust.	thrust.
tread.	trode.	trodden.
wear.	wore.	worn.
weave.	wove.	woven.
weep.	wept.	wept.
win.	won.	won.
wind.	wound.	wound.*
work.	wrought.	wrought.
wring.	wrung.	wrung.
write.	wrote.	written.

That

That this catalogue might be reduced
into as fmall a compafs as poffible, thofe
irregularities are omitted that have been
produced merely by the quick pronunciation of regular preterite tenfes and participles; whereby the *ed* is contracted into *t.* But this contraction is not admitted
in folemn language, except in verbs which
end in *l, ll,* or *p*; as *creep, crept; feel,
felt; dwell, dwelt;* though it is fometimes ufed in words ending in *d :* as *gird,
girt; geld, gelt,* &c.

****

NOTES,

AND

OBSERVATIONS,

For the Ufe of Thofe

Who have made fome. Profici
ency in the Language.

****

D 4

Notes

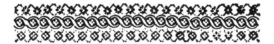

Notes and Obſervations,

For the Uſe of thoſe who have made
ſome Proficiency in the Language.

SECTION I.
Of the Plural Number of Nouns.

SOmetimes we find an apoſtrophe
uſed in the plural number, when
the noun ends in a vowel; as *in-
amorato's, toga's, tunica's, Otho's, a ſet of
virtuoſo's*. Addiſon on Medals. *The* idea's
*of the author have been converſant with the
faults of other writers.* Swift's Tale of a
Tub, p. 55. It is alſo uſed, ſometimes
when the noun ends in *s*; as, *genius's,
caduceus's, Jacobus's*. Addiſon on Medals,
p. 79. But it ſeems better to add *es* in
theſe caſes; as, *rendezvouſes*. Hume's
Hiſtory, vol. 7. p. 113.

D 3 Words

Words compounded of *man* have *men* in the plural; as, *Alderman, aldermen. Muſſulmans,* (Smollett's Voltaire, vol. 2. p. 58.) ſeems aukward.

Words derived from foreign languages often retain their original plural terminations; as, *Cherubim, phænomena, radii, beaux.* But when foreign words are completely incorporated into our language, they take Engliſh plurals, as *epitomes.* Addiſon. When words of foreign extraction are, as it were, half incorporated into the language, they ſometimes retain their native plurals, and ſometimes acquire thoſe of the Engliſh. Thus ſome perſons write *criterions,* others *criteria;* ſome write *mediums,* and others *media.* Some foreign words both retain their native plurals, and acquire the Engliſh, but they are uſed in different ſenſes. This is the caſe with the word *index.* We ſay *indexes* of books, and *indices* of algebraical quantities.

When a noun is compounded of an adjective, which has not entirely coaleſced with it into one word, it occaſions ſome difficulty where to place the ſign of the plural number, as in the word *handful.* Some would ſay *two hands full;* others, *two handfuls*; and Butler, perhaps for the fake of the rhyme, writes *two handful.*

> *For of the lower part,* two handful,
> *It had devoured, it was fo manful.*

When a name has a title prefixed to it, as *Doctor, Mifs, Mafter, &c.* the plural termination affects only the latter of the two words; as, *the two Doctor Nettletons, the two Mifs Thomfons*; tho' a ftrict analogy would plead for the alteration of the former word, and lead us to fay, *the two Doctors Nettleton, the two Miffes Thomfon :* for, if we fupplied the ellipfis, we fhould fay, *the two Doctors of the name of Nettleton;* and, *the two young ladies of the name of Thomfon ;* and I remember to have met with this conftruction fomewhere, either in Clariffa, or Sir Charles Grandifon; but I cannot now recollect the paffage.

Many of the words which have no fingular number, denote things which confift of two parts, or go by pairs, and therefore are, in fome meafure, intitled to a plural termination; as, *lungs, bellows, breeches.* The word *pair* is generally ufed with many of them; as *a pair of compaffes, a pair of drawers, a pair of colours, &c.* Alfo many of thefe words denote things which confift of many parts, and therefore are, in the

D 6　　　　　ftricteft

strifteft fenfe, plurals ; as *grains, annals,*
oats, mallows, and other plants ; *afhes,*
*embers, filings, vitals, hatcke*s, *cloaths, &c.*
But others are not eafily reduced to this
rule, and no reafon can be given why the
things might not have been expreffed by
words of the fingular number ; as, *calands,*
noues, ides, riches, odds, fhambles, thanks,
*tidings, wages, victua*ls, and things that
have only quantity, and do not exift in
diftinct parts ; as, *the grounds of liquors,*
beaftings, affets, &c.

Many of the words which have no fingular termination, are the names of fciences ; as, *ethics, mathematics, belles lettres,*
&c. Many of them are the names of
games ; as *billiards, fives,* &c. Many of
them, alfo, are the names of difeafes ; as
the *meafles, hifterics, glanders,* &c. And
fome, in imitation of the Greek and Latin,
are the names of feftivals, and other ftated
times ; as *orgies, matins, vefpers,* &c.

Some of thefe words have a fingular
termination in ufe, but it is applied in a
different fenfe ; as *arms,* for weapons, and
an *arm* of the body ; a pair of *colours* belonging to the army, good *manners,* a
perfon's *goods,* good *graces,* a foldier's
quarters, a man's *betters, hangings, doings.*
And of their doings *great diflike declared.*
                                        Milton.

Milton. Some words are alfo found in the fingular, but more generally in the plural; as *firft fruits, antipodes,* &c.

To exprefs the fingular of any of thefe words which have only a plural termination in ufe, we have recourfe to a periphrafis; as, *one of the annals, one of the grains, one of the pleiades,* &c.

Tradefmen fay *one pound, twenty pound,* &c. And the fame rule they obferve with refpeft to all weights and meafures. Alfo a gentleman will always fay, *how many carp,* or *how many tench,* &c. have you, and never *how many carps,* or *how many tenches,* &c. This may be faid to be ungrammatical; or, at leaft, a very harfh ellipfis; but cuftom authorizes it, and many more departures from ftrict grammar, particularly in converfation. Sometimes writers have adopted this colloquial form of fpeech. *He is faid to have fhot, with his own hands,* fifty brace *of pheafants.* Addifon. *When Innocent the 11th defired the Marquis de Eaftres to furnifh* thirty thoufand head *of fwine, he could not fpare them, but* thirty thoufand *lawyers he had at his fervice.* Addifon. *A fleet of* thirty-nine fail. *Hume's Hift. vol.* 3. *p.* 448.

Many words, however, in the fingular number, feem to be ufed in the plural
con-

conftruction ; when, perhaps, the fupplying of an ellipfis would make it pretty
eafy. *The Queen dowager became more a-
verfe to all alliance with a nation, who had
departed fo far from all ancient principles.*
Hume's Hift. vol. 4. p. 833. i. e. *all
kinds of alliance.* Thus we fay, *a thoufand
horfe, or foot* ; meaning a thoufand of the
troops that fight on foot, or with a horfe.
They are a good apple, i. e. they are of a
good fpecies of the fruit called *an apple.*
And thus, alfo, perhaps, may fome of
the examples in the former paragraph be
analized.

Names of mental qualities feldom have
any plurals, yet when particular acts and
not general habits are meant, the plural
number fometimes occurs ; as *infclences.*
Hume's Hift. vol. 7. p. 411. But it feems
better to have recourfe to a periphrafis
in this cafe. In things of an intellectual
nature, the fingular number will often
fuffice, even when the things fpoken of
are mentioned as belonging to a number
of perfons ; but if the things be corporeal,
though they be ufed in a figurative fenfe,
the plural number feems to be required.
Thus we fay, *their defign, their intention*,
and perhaps, *their heart* ; but not *their
head*, or *their mouth. This people draws
nigh*

nigh unto me with their mouth, *and honours me with* their lips, *but* their heart *is far from* me. Matthew. *Ferdinand designed to wrest from the Venetians some towns, which his predecessor had consigned to* their hand. Hume's Hist. vol. 3. p. 438.

Words that do not admit of a plural, on account of their being of an intellectual nature, are easily applied to a number of persons. Thus we say, *the courage of an army,* or *the courage of a thousand men;* though each man, separately taken, be supposed to have courage. In these cases, if we take away the abstract and intellectual term, and substitute another, which is particular and corporeal, we must change the number, though the construction and meaning of the sentence be the same. *The enmity of Fran is the first, and Charles the fifth, subsisted between* their posterity *for several ages.* Robertson's Hist. of Scotland, vol. 1. p. 74. If the author had not used the word *posterity,* which is in the singular number, he must have said *children,* or *sons,* or *descendants,* in the plural.

There are many words which, in general, have no plurals, as *wool, wheat,* &c. which people who are much conversant with the things which they signify, and who

who have occaſion to make more diſ-
tinctions among them, uſe in the plural
number, and ſometimes thoſe plurals get
into writing. *The* coarſer wools *have
their uſes alſo.* Preceptor, vol 2. p. 435.
Yet when nouns, which have uſually no
plurals, are uſed in that number, the effect is very diſagreeable. *But one of the*
principal foods *uſed by the inhabitants is
cheeſe.* Ulloa's Voyage, vol. 1. p. 304.
This conſtruction might eaſily have been
avoided by a periphraſis ; as, *but one of
the principal kinds of food, &c.*

The word *means* belongs to the claſs of
words which do not change their termination on account of number ; for it is uſed
alike in both numbers. *Leſt* this means
ſhould fail. Hume's Hiſtory, vol. 8. p. 65.
Some perſons, however, uſe the ſingular
of this word, and would ſay, *leſt* this mean
ſhould fail, and Dr. Lowth pleads for it ;
but cuſtom has ſo formed our ears, that
they do not eaſily admit this form of the
word, notwithſtanding it is more agreeable
to the general analogy of the language.

The word *pains* is alſo uſed in the
ſingular number ; *No* pains is *taken* ;
Great pains has *been taken.* Pope. But
both this, and the word *means,* are alſo
uſed as plurals.

The

The word *news* is alfo ufed both in the fingular and plural number. *Pray, Sir,* are *there any* news *of bis intimate friend and confident Darmin.* Smollett's Voltaire, vol. 18. p. 131. News were *brought to the Queen.* Hume's Hiftory, vol. 4. p. 426. Are *there any* news *at prefent ftirring in London.* Englifh Merchant, p. 7. But notwithftanding thofe authorities, the fingular number feems to be more common, and is therefore to be preferred.

The word *billet-doux* is alfo ufed in both numbers. *Her eyes firft opened on* a billet-doux. Pope's Rape of the Lock.— *Will be carrying about* billet-doux. Arbuthnot.

In fome cafes we find two plurals in ufe. The word *brother* is an example of this; for we both fay *brothers,* and *brethren;* but the former is ufed of natural relations, and the other in a figurative fenfe; as, *men and brethren.* The word *die,* which makes *dice* when it relates to gaming, makes *dies,* in the plural number, when it relates to coin. The word *cow* formerly had *kine* in the plural number, but we now fay *cows.* The word *Sir* has hardly any plural, except in very folemn ftyle, borrowed from the old ufe

of

of it, as, Oh, Sirs, *what ſhall I do to be ſaved.* Acts.

Both the word *fclk*, and *folks* ſeem to be uſed promiſcuouſly, eſpecially in converſation; as when we ſay, *where are the good folks,* or *folk* ; but the latter ſeems to be preferable, as the word in the ſingular form implies a number.

Proper names admit of a plural number, where they are figuratively uſed for common names. *It is not enough to have* Vitruviuſes, *we muſt alſo have* Auguſtuſes, to employ them. Smollett's Voltaire, vol, 9. p. 27.

It is indifferent, in ſome caſes, whether we uſe a word in the ſingular, or in the plural number. Thus we ſay *in hopes,* or *in hope,* and in the very ſame ſenſe. *His old inſtructor, imagining that he had now made himſelf acquainted with his diſeaſe of mind, was* in hope *of curing it.* Raſſelas, vol. 1. p. 16. *They went* their ways. Matthew. We ſhould now ſay, *went their* way; but, in the Yorkſhire dialect, it is ſtill, *went their* ways. *The laſt Pope was at conſiderable* charges. Addiſon. *Notwithſtanding the ravages of theſe two inſatiable enemies,* their numbers *can hardly be imagined.* Ulloa's voyage, vol, 4. p. 202.

p. 202. *Their number* would exprefs the
whole idea, but perhaps not with the
fame emphafis. The fingular number
would have been better than the plural,
in the following fentence,—*putting cur
minds into the* difpofals *of others.* Locke.

Section II.

*Of the Genitive Cafe, and other In-
flexions of Nouns.*

IT may feem improper to call the *Nominative* a *cafe* (i. e. *cafus, five inflectio*)
which is the root from whence other cafes
are derived; but the practice of all Grammarians, and the long eftablifhed definition of terms, authorize this deviation
from rigid exactnefs.

The [*f*] at the end of a word, doth
not change into [*v*] for the genitive cafe,
as it doth in the plural number. We
fay *a* wife's *fortune*; but, *he takes more*
wives *than one*.

The *apoftrophe* denotes the omiffion of
an [*i*] which was formerly inferted, and
made an addition of a fyllable to the
word.

word.——Mr. *Pope*, and fome of his cotemporaries, to avoid a harfhnefs in the
pronunciation of fome genitives, wrote
the word [*his*] at the end of the word;
as *Statius his Thebais, Socrates his fetters*
(Spect.) imagining the [*'s*] to be a contraction for that pronoun : But analogy
eafily overturns that fuppofition; for *Venus his beauty*, or *Men his wit*, were ab-
furd.

The genitive neceffarily occafions the
addition of a fyllable to words ending
in [*s*], and the other terminations which
have the fame effect in the plural number; as *Venus's beauty, Mofes's rod*. Sometimes the additional [*s*] is fuppreffed in
writing, and nothing but the apoftrophe
remains. *And caft him down at* Jefus'
feet. But this is more common with poets, when the additional fyllable would
have been more than their verfe required.

Sometimes the apoftrophe is wholly
omitted, even after the plural number;
tho', in that cafe, there is no other fign
of the genitive cafe. *A collection of* writers *faults*. Swift's Tale of a Tub, p. 55.
After ten years *wars*. Swift.

When, in this and other cafes, the terminations of words are fuch, that the found
makes no diftinction between the genitive

of the fingular and of the plural number;
as, *the prince's injuries,* and *prince's injuries.*
Humes s Hift, vol. 5. p. 406. It fhould
feem to be better to decline the ufe of
the genitive in the plural number, and
fay, *the injuries of princes.*

The Englifh genitive has often a very
harfh found, fo that, in imitation of the
French, we daily make more ufe of the
particle, *of,* as they do of *de,* to exprefs
the fame relation. There is fomething
aukward in the following fentences, in
which this method has not been taken.
The general, in the army's name, *publifhed
a declaration.* Hume. *The Commons' vote.*
Hume's Hiftory, vol. 8. p. 217. *The
Lords' houfe.* Id. *Unlefs he be very ignorant of* the kingdom's condition. Swift.
It were certainly better to fay, *In the
name of the army, the votes of the Commons,
the houfe of Lords, the condition of the kingdom.* Befides, *the Lord's houfe,* which is
the fame in found with *Lords' Houfe,* is
an expreffion almoft appropriated to a
place fet apart for chriftian worfhip.

When an entire claufe of a fentence,
beginning with a participle of the prefent
tenfe, is ufed as one name, or to exprefs
one idea, or circumftance, the noun on
which it depends may be put in the genitive

nitive cafe. Thus, inftead of faying, *What is the meaning of this lady holding up her train*, i. e. *what is the meaning of the lady in holding up her train*, we may fay, *What is the meaning of this* lady's *holding up her train* ; juft as we fay, *What is the meaning of this lady's drefs, &c.* So we may either fay, *I remember* it being *reckoned a great exploit* ; or, perhaps more elegantly, *I remember* its being *reckoned, &c.*

When a name is complex, confifting of more terms than one, the genitive is made by fubjoining the [*s*] to the laft of the terms. *For Herodias' fake, his brother Philip's wife.* Matthew. *Lord Feverfham the general's tent.* Hume's Hiftory, vol. 8. p. 264. This conftruction, however, often feems to be aukward. It would have been eafier and better to have faid, *The tent of Lord Feverfham the general, &c.* When a term confifts of a name, and an office, or any term explanatory of the former, it may occafion fome doubt to which of them the fign of the genitive fhould be annexed, or whether it fhould be fubjoined to them both. Thus, fome would fay, *I left the parcel at Mr. Smith's the bookfeller* ; others, *at Mr. Smith the bookfeller's*, and perhaps others, *at Mr. Smith's the bookfeller's.* The laft of thefe
forms

forms is moft agreeable to the Latin idiom, but the firft feems to be more natural in ours ; and if the addition confift of two or more words, the cafe feems to be very clear ; as, *I left the parcel at Mr. Smith's the bookfeller and ftationer*, *i. e.* at Mr. Smith's, who is a bookfeller and ftationer, tho' the relative does not eafily follow a genitive cafe.

It is by no means elegant to ufe two Englifh genitives in conftruction with the fame noun. *He fummoned an affembly of bifhops and abbots, whom he acquainted with* the pope's *and the* king's pleafure. Hume's Hiftory; vol. 2. p. 177. *The pleafure of the pope, and the king*, would have been better.

In fome cafes we ufe both the genitive and the prepofition *of*; as, *this book of my friend's.* Sometimes, indeed, this method is quite neceffary, in order to diftinguifh the fenfe, and to give the idea of property, ftrictly fo called, which is the moft important of the relations expreffed by a genitive cafe. *This picture of my friend*, and *this picture of my friend's*, fuggeft very different ideas. The latter only is that of property in the ftricteft fenfe. Where this double genitive, as it may be called, is not neceffary to diftinguifh the fenfe, and

and efpecially in grave ftyle, it is generally omitted. Thus we fay, *It is a difcovery of Sir Ifaac Newton*, tho' it would
not have been improper, only more familiar, to fay *It is a difcovery of Sir Ifaac
Newton's*. That this double genitive is
fufficiently agreeable to the analogy of
the Englifh language, is evident from the
ufual conjunction of the pronoun poffeffive with the prepofition *of*, both of
which have the force of a genitive. *This
exactnefs of his*. Triftram Shandy, vol. 1.
p. 12. In reality, this double genitive
may be refolved into two; for, *this is a
book of my friend's*, is the fame as, *this is
one of the books of my friend*.

The Englifh modification of a word,
to exprefs the feminine gender, extends
not to many words in our language, and
the analogy fails when we fhould moft
expect it would be kept up. Thus we
do not call a female author, an *authorefs*;
and if a lady write poems, fhe is now-a-
days called a *poet*, rather than a *poetefs*,
which is almoft obfolete.

A few of our feminine terminations
are Latin, with little or no variation, as
adminiftrator, *adminiftratrix*; *director*, *di-
rectrix*; *hero*, *heroine*.

†

The

The mafculine gender is fometimes
expreffed by prefixing words which are
known to be the names of males; as,
a *dog-fox*, *jack-afs*, &c. but generally the
mafculine is denoted by *he*, and the fe-
mine by *fhe*; as, *he-fox*, *fhe-fox*.

SECTION III.

Of Adjectives.

THE adjective *enough* may be faid to
have a plural in our language; for
we fay *enough* with refpect to quantity,
which is fingular; and *enow* with refpect
to number, which is plural. *I think
there are at Rome* enow *modern works of
architecture.* Addifon. *There are* enow
of zealots of both fides. Hume's Effays,
p. 32.

The word *every* is by fome writers
tranfpofed, and connected with the perfonal pronouns, in a manner that feems to
found harfh to an Englifh ear.

Palmira, thou command'ft my *every*
thought, i. e. *all my thoughts.* Smollett's
Voltaire, vol. 25. pag. 82.

My

My ev'ry thought, *my* ev'ry hope *is fix'd*
On him alone. Ib. vol. 18. p. 10.

The which conduct, throughout every, its·
minuteſt energy. Harris's three Treatiſes, p. 189.

Some adjectives of number are more
eaſily converted into ſubſtantives than o-
thers. Thus we more eaſily ſay *a million*
of men, than *a thouſand of men.* On the
other hand, it will hardly be admitted to
ſay *a million men*; whereas *a thouſand men*
is quite familiar. Yet, in the plural number, a different conſtruction ſeems to be
required. We ſay *ſome hundreds,* or *thou-*
ſands, as well as *millions of men.* Perhaps,
on this account, the words *million, hun-*
dreds, and *thouſands* will be ſaid to·be ſubſtantives.

In numbering we often reckon by twen-
ties, calling them *ſcores*; *as three ſcore,*
four ſcore, tho' we never ſay *two ſcore.*

In ſome few caſes we ſeem, after the
manner of the Greeks, to make the adjective agree with the ſubject of the affirmation; when, in ſtrictneſs, it belongs
to ſome other word in the ſentence; as,
you had better do it; for, *it would be better*
for you to do it.

An adjective and a ſubſtantive are both
united in the word *aught,* put for *any thing,*
and

and *naught* put for *nothing*. *For aught which to me appears contrary.* Harris's three Treatiſes, p. 21. *Naught was wanting.* Hume's Hiſtory, vol. 6. p. 5. Theſe contraſtions, however, are but little uſed, and are hardly to be approved of.

The word *leſſer*, though condemned by Mr. Johnſon, and other Engliſh grammarians, is often uſed by good writers. *The greater number frequently fly before the* leſſer. Smollett's Voltaire, vol. 1. p. 172. *The kings of France were the chief of ſeveral greater vaſſals, by whom they were very ill obeyed, and of a greater number of* leſſer *ones.* Ib. vol. 6. p. 172.

Sometimes the comparative of *late* is written *latter*, as well as *later*; and, I think, we uſe thoſe two comparatives in different ſenſes. The *latter of two*, I fancy, refers either to place or time, whereas *later* reſpeſts time only.

In ſeveral adjeſtives the termination *moſt* is uſed to expreſs the ſuperlative degree; as, *hindermoſt*, or *hindmoſt*; *hithermoſt* (almoſt obſolete); *uppermoſt*, *undermoſt*, *nethermoſt*, *innermoſt*, *outermoſt*, *uttermſt* or *utmoſt*. Some of theſe have no comparatives, or poſitives, or none that are adjeſtives.

The

The adjective *old* is compared two ways. We both say *older*, and *oldeſt*; and like-wiſe, *elder*, and *eldeſt*; but uſe ſeems to have aſſigned to them different accepta-tions; for *elder*, and *eldeſt* ſeem to refer to priority of rank or privilege, in conſe-quence of age; whereas *older* and *oldeſt*, reſpect the number of years only. Speak-ing of two very old perſons, we ſhould naturally ſay, that one of them was the *older of the two*; but ſpeaking of two bro-thers, with reſpect to the right of inherit-ance, we ſhould ſay, that one of them was *the elder of the two.*

Several adverbs are uſed, in an elegant manner, to anſwer the purpoſe of degrees of compariſon. There is great beauty in the uſe of the word *rather*, to expreſs a ſmall degree, or exceſs of a quality. *She is ra-ther profuſe in her expences.* Critical Re-view, N° 90. p. 43.

The word *full* is likewiſe uſed to ex-preſs a ſmall exceſs of any quality. Thus we ſay, *The tea is* full *weak*, or full *ſtrong*; but this is only a colloquial phraſe.

The prepoſition *with* is alſo ſometimes uſed in converſation, to expreſs a degree of quality ſomething leſs than the great-eſt; as, *They are with the wideſt.*

Some-

Sometimes comparatives are used in a sense merely positive, so that it may occasion a little surprize to find them used in a sense strictly comparative; as the phrase *wiser and better* in the following sentence. *It is a glorious privilege, and he, who practises it, may grow* wiser and better *by an hour's serious meditation, than by a month's reading.* Female American, vol. 1. p. 103.

There are some *Dissyllables* which would not admit the termination [*er*] or [*est*] without a harshness in the pronunciation. It is, therefore, usual to compare them in the same manner as *Polysyllables*, without any change of termination. Of these, Mr. *Johnson* has given us the following enumeration; viz. such as terminate in,

some, as *fulsome.*	*ive*, as *massive.*
ful, as *careful.*	*dy*, as *woody.*
ing, as *trifling.*	*fy*, as *puffy.*
ous, as *porous.*	*ky*, as *rocky*; except
less, as *careless.*	*lucky.*
ed, as *wretched.*	*my*, as *roomy.*
id, as *candid.*	*ny*, as *skinny.*
al, as *mortal.*	*py*, as *ropy*; except
ent, as *recent.*	*happy.*
ain, as *certain.*	*ry*, as *hoary.*

Some

Some adjectives do not, in their own nature, and by reafon of their fignification, admit of comparifon ; fuch as *univerfal*, *perfect*, &c. yet it is not uncommon to fee the comparative or fuperlative of fuch words ; being ufed, either thro' inadvertency, or for the fake of emphafis. *He fometimes claims admiffion to the* chiefeft *officers of the army.* Clarendon. *The quarrel was become* fo univerfal *and national.* Hume's Hiftory, vol. 1. p. 258. *A method of attaining* the righteft *and greateft happinefs.* Price.

There is ftill a greater impropriety in a double comparative, or a double fuperlative. Dr. Lowth thinks there is a fingular propriety in the phrafe *moft higheft*, which is peculiar to the old tranflation of the Pfalms. But I own it offends my ears, which may, perhaps, be owing to my not having been accuftomed to that tranflation.

It is very common to fee the fuperlative ufed for the comparative degree, when only two perfons or things are fpoken of. *It began to be the intereft of their neighbours, to oppofe the ftrongeft and moft enterprifing of the two.* Bolingbroke on Hiftory, vol. 1. p. 231. This is a very pardonable overfight.

In

In converfation, I do not fay the moſt polite, we fometimes hear the word *only*, which is a diminutive, joined to the fuperlative degree ; as, *He is* only the clevereſt *fellow I ever faw.* Originally, this form of expreſſion might have been defigned to expreſs ridicule, or contempt for a perſon who had undervalued another. It is now uſed, when no reply is made to any thing faid before, but in an affected, oſtentatious way of ſpeaking.

In fome cafes we find fubſtantives, without any alteration, uſed for adjectives, *In the* flux condition *of human affairs.* Bolingbroke on Hiſtory, vol. 1. p. 199. *A muſlin flounce, made very full, would give a very agreeable* flirtation air. Pope. *Chance companions.* Of this kind are, *an alabaſter column, a ſilver tankard, a grammar fchool,* and moſt other compound nouns.

Engliſh writers, agreeable to the well known idiom of the language, generally write *Scottiſh*, juſt as we fay Spaniſh, Iriſh, &c. and fometimes it is contracted into *Scotch*; but Mr. Hume always uſes the fubſtantive *Scots* inſtead of it. *The Scots commiſſioners.* Hiſtory, vol. 3. p. 379.

The fubſtantive *plenty*, is frequently uſed for the adjective *plentiful. In the reign of Henry the* 2d, *all foreign commo-*
dities

dities were plenty *in England.* Poftle-thwaite on Commerce, p. 414. i. e. were plentiful, or in plenty.

Names of towns and places, by the fame kind of ellipfis, are very often ufed for adjectives. Thus we fpeak of *our London*, or *Jamaica friends* ; i. e. meaning our friends in London or Jamaica.

When the name of a country cannot eafily be transformed into an adjective, it feems the beft to make ufe of the pre-pofition *of. The noblemen of Bretaigne* would, I think, be better than the *Bretaigne noblemen.* Hume's Hiftory, vol. 2. p. 433.

The word *friends* is ufed as an adjective in the phrafe, *Will you* be friends *with me.* Perfian Tales, vol. 2. p. 248. *i. e.* friendly, or in friendfhip with me.

Adjectives are often put for adverbs, but the practice is hardly to be approved, except in cafes where long cuftom has made the examples quite eafy ; as, *exceeding* for *exceedingly*, *near* for *nearly. Our wealth being near finifhed.* Harris's three Treatifes, p. 43. The following examples are not fo eafy. *The people are* miferable *poor, and fubfift on fifh. Extreme jealous.* Hume's Effays, p. 11. The word *exceeding* makes a worfe adjective than it
does

does·an adverb. *I was taking a view of Weſtminſter-abbey, with an old gentleman of* exceeding honeſty, *but the ſame degree of underſtanding, as that I have deſcribed.* Shenſtone's Works, vol. 2. p. 45. It ſhould have been exceeding great honeſty.

Like ſeems to be put for *likely*, in the following ſentence : *What the conſequences of this management are like to be* ; i. e. *what they are* likely *to be*, or *what they are*, according to all probability, *to be*.

SECTION IV.

Of Pronouns.

I. *Of Pronouns in general.*

IT might not have been improper to have claſſed all the *Pronouns* under the heads of *Subſtantives* or *Adjectives* ; the *perſonal* pronouns being of the former kind, and all the other denominations of the latter. The reaſon why they are conſidered ſeparately is, becauſe there is ſomething particular in their inflections. By this means therefore, the rules relating to *ſubſtantives* and *adjectives* in general, are

ren-

rendered more fimple, and a more diftinct
view is given of the irregular inflections
of thofe words which have been ufually
called *Pronouns*.

I, is called the *firft* perfon ; *Thou*, the
fecond ; and *He*, *She*, or *It*, the *third*
perfon.

By the complaifance of modern times,
we ufe the plural *you* inftead of the fingular *thou*, when we mean to fpeak refpectfully to any perfon ; but we do not ufe
ye in this manner. We fay *you*, not *ye*,
are reading. However, in very folemn
ftyle, and particularly in an addrefs to the
Divine Being, we ufe *thou*, and not *you*.

In fpeaking to children, we fometimes
ufe the third perfon fingular, inftead of
the fecond ; as, *will he*, or *fhe* do it.
The Germans ufe the third perfon plural,
when they fpeak the moft refpectfully.

The pronouns *you*, and *your* are fometimes ufed with little regard to their proper meaning ; for the fpeaker has juft as
much intereft in the cafe as thofe he ad-
dreffes. This ftyle is oftentatious, and doth
not fuit grave writing. *Not only* your *men of*
more refined and folid parts and learning, but
even your *alchymift, and* your *fortune teller,*
will difcover the fecrets of their art in Homer
and Virgil. Addifon on Medals, p. 32.

For

For want of a fufficient variety of perfonal pronouns of the third perfon, we are often obliged, in a complex fentence, to have recourfe to explanations which cannot be introduced without appearing very aukward. *Perigrine fpoke not a word in anfwer to this declaration, which he immediately imputed to the ill offices of the minifter againft whom he breathed defiance and revenge, in his way to the lodgings of Cadwalader ; who, being made acquainted with the manner of his reception, begged he would defift from all fchemes of vengeance, until he* (Crabtree) *fhould be able to unriddle the myftery of the whole.* Perigrine Pickle, vol. 4. p. 129. *In confequence of this retreat he,* (the hufband) *was difabled from paying a confiderable fum.* Ib. p. 242.

Aukward as this conftruction is, it were to be wifhed, that hiftorians had made more ufe of it ; as, at leaft, they would have been more intelligible than they fometimes are without it. *They* [meaning the French] *marched precipitately, as to an affured victory ; whereas the Englifh advanced very flowly, and d fcharged fuch flights of arrows, as did gre.t execution. When* they *drew near, the archers, perceiving that* they *were out of breath, charged* them *with great vigour.* Univerfal Hift.

vol. 23. p. 517. If an attention to the sense, in these cases, would relieve the ambiguity, yet the attention it requires is painful, and difficult to be kept up.

The pronoun *it* is sometimes used at the same time with the word for which it might have been substituted, and even precedes it; tho' such a word is generally called the antecedent of the pronoun. It is *our duty to do to others as we would that they should do to us.* If this complex antecedent, which is the proper nominative case to the verb *is,* be made to precede that verb, the pronoun will be superfluous, and the sentence will read thus, *To do to others, as we would that they should do to us, is our duty.*

This construction of the pronoun *it* is so common, and we so naturally expect the antecedent to follow it, or to be understood after it; that when the antecedent comes regularly before it, as before any other pronoun, the sense is, sometimes, in danger of being mistaken. *Who* [meaning the king] *notwithstanding he relates, that the prudent foresight of the commons had cut off all the means, whereby Charles could procure money, those nerves of power without which,* it is impossible *to exist.* Macaulay's History, vol. 3. p. 2. The phrase, phrafe, *it is impoffible to exift*, gives us the idea of it's being impoffible for men, or any body to exift; whereas, *power* is the thing that the author meant could not exift without money.

Sometimes the true antecedent of this pronoun is fo concealed in other words, that it requires fome attention to difcover it. *How far do you call* it *to fuch a place? You will have* it *to be three miles.* That is, *how great a diftance do you call it? You will have the diftance to be three miles.*

Not only things, but perfons may be the antecedent to this pronoun. *Who is it? Is it not Thomas?* i. e. *Who is the perfon? Is not he Thomas?*

Sometimes, in imitation of the French, this pronoun may be ufed for a perfon in another manner, by being fubftituted for *he. What a defperate fellow* it *is.* But this is only in converfation, and familiar ftyle.

In one very odd phrafe, which alfo occurs in converfation, efpecially in fome counties of England, the pronoun *it* is put in the place of a perfonal pronoun, and the perfonal pronoun in the place of it. *He put him into the head of it. It is upon a fubject perfectly new, and thofe dogs there put me into the head of it.* Pom-
pey

pey the Little, p. 246. in ridicule of the phrafe.

Sometimes this fame pronoun connects fo clofely with the verb, that it feems only to modify its meaning, and not to have any feparate fignification of its own. *The king carried* it *with a high hand.* Parliamentary Hiftory, vol. 1. p. 14. i. e. *the king behaved with haughtinefs.*

If there be any antecedent in fome fuch phrafes as thefe, it is fuch a complex idea, that I do not think it is poffible to give a precife definition of it. I fhall fubjoin a curious example of this. *Let me beg of you, like an unbacked filly, to frifk* it, *to fquirt* it, *to jump* it, *to rear* it, *to bound* it, *and to kick* it, *with long kicks, and fhort kicks, till you break the ftrap or a crupper, and throw his worfhip into the dirt.* Triftram Shandy, vol. 3. p. 167.

The pronouns *poffeffive* [indicating *property* or *poffeffion*] might not improperly have been called the *genitive* cafes of their correfponding *perfonal* pronouns, were it not that their formation is not analogous to that of the genitive cafes of other words.

Sometimes thefe poffeffives have an apoftrophe before the *s,* when they are found without their fubftantives, which gives
them

them more the appearance of a genitive cafe. *That you may call her your's.* Fair American, vol. 2. p. 64.

Formerly, *mine* and *thine* were ufed inftead of *my* and *thy* before a vowel. They are generally retained in our prefent Englifh verfion of the Bible; and, perhaps, for this reafon, give a peculiar folemnity to the ftyle. *By the greatnefs of thine arm.* Exodus, ch. 15. ver. 16. *And bring them to thine everlafting kingdom.* Common Prayer.

The pronoun *his* was not always confined to perfons, but was formerly applied to things alfo. *This rule is not fo general, but that it admitteth his exceptions.* Carew.

For want of a fufficient variety of perfonal pronouns of the third perfon, and their poffeffives, our language labours under an ambiguity, which is unknown in moft others. *The eagle killed the hen, and eat her in* her own *neft. He fent him to kill* his own *father.* Nothing but the fenfe of the preceding fentences can determine what neft, the *hen's*, or the *eagle's*, is meant in the former of thefe examples; or whofe father, his that gave the order, or his that was to execute it, in the latter.

Some-

Sometimes thefe pronouns poffeffive **do** not ftrictly imply property, and on this account occafion an ambiguity in a fentence. *But is it poffible 1 fhould not grieve for* his lofs ? Fair American, vol. 1. p. 38. Meaning the lofs of her father, who was dead ; but the meaning might have been a lofs which her father had fuftained.

According to the Englifh idiom, we generally prefix the pronoun *my* to the title of *Lord*; as *my Lord Bedford*, but this ftyle feems to imply fome degree of familiarity ; and perfons who pretend not to any fort of intimacy with the nobility, do not commonly ufe it. Indeed it feems proper to the ftyle of a king, whofe Lords they originally were, and whofe manner it is to fay, *my fubjects, my kingdom, my Lords and gentlemen, my fhips, my army, &c.* Foreigners often confound this pronoun with the word *Lord*, as if they made but one word ; as, *a mylord.*

When the relative is preceded by two perfonal pronouns, as antecedents, it may, in fome cafes, relate to the former, and in others to the latter of them, according as the fenfe may point out its reference, but it is generally the latter that is referred to ; as *I am he that liveth, and was dead :* where the antecedent of *that* is *he*, which immediately precedes it ; *he that liveth* being confidered as one idea, or character, to which the perfon intended by *I* anfwers. Yet, *I am he, that live, and was dead*, could hardly be condemned, if it be confidered, who it is that liveth, viz. *I.*

When the relative follows two nouns, connected by the particle *of*, it is abfolutely impoffible to fay, to which of them it refers ; becaufe the cuftom of the language has made it equally applicable to either of them. When we fay, *the difciples of Chrift*, whom *we imitate*, we may mean the imitation either of Chrift, or of his difciples. Here we find the want of a diftinction of numbers, in the pronoun relative.

When the words are feparated by other prepofitions, there is, fometimes, the fame ambiguity. *He was taking a view, from a window of St. Chad's cathedral, in Litchfield, where* [i. e. in which] *a party of the royalifts had fortified themfelves.* Hume's Hiftory, vol. 6. p. 449. Quere, was it in the cathedral, or in the town, that the party of the royalifts were fortified ?

The pronouns *Relative* and *Demonftrative* are nearly allied ; every pronoun *demon-*

monſtrative, when not immediately preceding a ſubſtantive, referring to an *antecedent* one; as alſo do the *poſſeſſives*: And, being all of the nature of *adjectives*, it is impoſſible it ſhould be otherwiſe.

The pronouns *demonſtrative* are ſo called, becauſe when we make uſe of them we, as it were, *point out* the thing that we ſpeak of; for ſuch is the import of the word [*demonſtro*] from which the term is derived.

The demonſtrative *this* refers to the nearer, or the laſt mentioned particular, and *that* to the more remote, or the firſt mentioned. *More rain falls in June and July, than in December and January; but it makes a much greater ſhow upon the earth in* theſe *than in* thoſe; *becauſe it lies longer upon it.* Woodward.

The pronoun *this*, or *thoſe*, without the relative and verb ſubſtantive, but ill ſupplies the place of a noun ſubſtantive, which ought to be its antecedent. *The land was always poſſeſſed, during pleaſure, by* thoſe *intruſted with the command.* Hume's Hiſtory, vol. 5. p. 109. i. e. *thoſe perſons intruſted, or thoſe who were intruſted. All* thoſe *poſſeſſed of any office reſigned their former commiſſion.* Hume's Hiſtory, vol. 4. p. 304.

Many

Many perfons are apt, in converfation, to put the oblique cafe of the perfonal pronouns, in the place of *thefe* and *thofe*; as, *Give me them books*, inftead of *thofe books*. We may, fometimes, find this fault even in writing. *Obferve* them three there. Devil upon Crutches.

It is not, however, always eafy to fay, whether a perfonal pronoun or a demonftrative is preferable in certain conftructions. *We are not unacquainted with the calumny of* them [*or* thofe] *who openly make ufe of the warmeft profeffions.* Preceptor, vol. 2. p. 429.

The demonftrative *that*, is fometimes ufed very emphatically for *fo much. But the circulation of things, occafioned by commerce, is not of* that *moment as the tranfplantation, which human nature itfelf has undergone,* Spirit of Nations, p. 22.

Sometimes this fame pronoun is elegantly ufed for *fo great*, or *fuch a. Some of them have gone to* that *height of extravagance, as to affert, that that performance had been immediately dictated by the holy ghoft.* Hume's Hiftory, vol. 5. p. 288. *It muft reafonably appear doubtful, whether human fociety could ever arrive at* that *ftate of perfection, as to fupport itfelf with no other control, than the general and rigid maxims*

of

of law and equity. Hume's Hiſtory, vol. 8.
p. 3 7. In all theſe caſes, however, it
ſhould ſeem, that the common conſtruction is generally preferable.

Sometimes this pronoun is introduced
in the latter part of a ſentence ; where it
is ſuperfluous with reſpect to the grammar,
and where it has no direct antecedent ;
but where it is of conſiderable uſe in point
of emphaſis. *By what arguments he cou d*
engage the French to offer ſuch an inſult to
the Spaniſh nation, from whom he met with
ſuch generous treatment ; by what colours he
could diſguiſe the ingratitude, and impudence
of ſuch a meaſure ; theſe *are wholly unknown*
to us. Hume's Hiſtory, vol. 6. p. 59.
As to the preciſe and definite idea, this *may*
be ſtill a ſecret. Harris's three Treatiſes,
p. 5.

The word *what* is a contraction for
that which, and therefore ſhould not be
uſed inſtead of *which* only. *Beſides, it*
happens, with regard to ambitious aims and
projects, what *may be obſerved with regard*
to ſects of philoſophy and religion: Hume's
Eſſays, p. 74. This ſentence can no otherwiſe be reduced to ſufficient correctneſs
than by reading, *it happens—which.* *I*
would not willingly inſiſt upon it as an ad-
vantage, in our European cuſtoms, what *was*
                                        obſerved

obſerved by Mahomet Effendi, the laſt Turkiſh
ambaſſador in France. Ib. p. 252.

In ſome dialects, the word *what* is uſed
for *that*; and ſometimes we find it in this
ſenſe in writing. *Neither Lady Haverſham*
nor Miſs Mildmay will ever believe, but
what *I have been entirely to blame.* Louiſa
Mildmay, vol 1. p. 179. *I am not ſatis-*
fied, but what *the integrity of · our friends is*
more eſſential to our welfare than their know-
ledge of the world. Ib. vol. 2. p. 114.

What is ſometimes put for *all the,* or
words nearly equivalent. What *appear-*
ances of worth afterwards ſucceeded, were
drawn from thence. Internal Policy of
Great Britain, p. 196. i. e. *all the appear-*
ances.

The word *other* ſeems to be uſed like
an adjective in the comparative degree
requiring *than* after it; but then it ſhould
have *a, any,* or ſome word equivalent to
the article before it. *Such inſtitutions are·*
too diabolical, to be derived from other *than*
an infernal demon. Hume's Hiſtory. vol. 6.
p. 24. i. e. *from any other. He frequently*
paſſed whole days in a hollow tree, without
other *company, or amuſement, than his Bible.*
Ib. vol. 7. p. 342.

When this pronoun is ſeparated from
its ſubſtantive, which follows it, by nothing

thing but the particle *of*, not having the force of a genitive cafe, or implying pof-feffion, but merely explanatory, as it may be called; it may, I think, be doubted, whether the plural *s*, fhould be added to it, or not. *The fons of Zebedee, and two other of his difciples.* John, ch. 2 1. v. 2. Some might write, *two others of his difci-ples*, i. e. *two others, who were his difciples*, or *among his difciples*.

The word *fomewhat*, in the following fentence of Hume, feems to be ufed im-properly. *Thefe punifhments feem to have been exercifed in* fomewhat *an arbitrary manner.* Hiftory, vol. 1. p. 371. Some-times we read, *in fomewhat of.* The mean-ing is, *in a manner which is, in fome refpects, arbitrary.*

The word *one* hath alfo a *pronominal* ufe, and may then be as properly claffed among the *Demonftratives* as *other* and *the fame*; as, *He is* one *that I efteem.* One *might make a magazine of all forts of antiquities.* Addifon.

We fometimes ufe the pronoun *one* in the fame fenfe in which *on* is ufed in French. One *would imagine thefe to be the expreffions of a man bleffed with eafe.* At-terbury.

This

This pronoun *one* has a plural number, when it is ufed without a fubftantive.
*There are many whofe waking thoughts are
wholly employed in their fleeping* ones. Addifon.

I fhall here mention a remarkable ambiguity in the ufe of the word *one,* when it
is no pronoun. And it is fuch as, I think,
cannot be avoided, except by a periphrafis, in any language. *I cannot find* one *of
my books.* By thefe words I may either
mean, that all the books are miffing, or
only one of them ; but the tone of voice,
with which they are fpoken, will eafily
diftinguifh in this cafe.

The word *none* has, generally, the force
of a pronoun ; as, *Where are the books ?
I have* none *of them.* In this cafe, it feems
to be the fame word with the adjective
no ; for where *no* is ufed with the fubftantive, *none* is ufed without it : for we fay,
I have no books ; or, *I have none.* This
word is ufed in a very peculiar fenfe. *If-
rael would* none *of me. I like* none *of it.*
i. e. would not have me at all ; do not
like it at all.

Under the article of *Pronouns* the following words and parts of words, that are
often joined with pronouns to increafe their
emphafis, muft be taken notice of. By
the

the addition of *foever* ; *who* and *what* become *whofoever* and *whatfoever.* The
indeclinable particle *own* added to the
poffeffives makes *my*, *thy*, *&c.* become
my own, *thy own*, *&c.* *Self* and its plural
number, *felves*, are added likewife to the
poffeffives, and fometimes to the oblique
cafes of the *perfonal* pronouns ; as *myfelf*,
yourfelves, *himfelf*, *themfelves* ; and, laftly,
the article [*a*] joined to the fimple pronoun *other*, makes it the compound *another.*

Hisfelf, and *theirfelves*, were formerly
ufed for *himfelf* and *themfelves.* *Every
one of us*, *each for hisfelf*, *laboured how to
recover him.* Sydney.

Ourfelf is peculiar to the royal ftyle ;
for the king only can properly make
ufe of it. *We* ourfelf *will follow.* Shake-
fpeare.

II. *Of Pronouns Relative.*

Formerly the words *who* and *which* were ufed without diftinction; but cuftom hath now appropriated *who* to *perfons*, and *which* to *things*.

It is not neceffary that the relative *who* have an exprefs perfonal antecedent. It is fufficient if it be implied in the pronoun poffeffive; as, thy *goodnefs* who *art*, i. e. *the goodnefs of thee who art*.

This pronoun, however, is fo much appropriated to perfons, that there is generally harfhnefs in the application of it, except to the proper names of perfons, or the general terms, man, woman, &c. A term which only implies the idea of perfons, and expreffes them by fome circumftance or epithet, will hardly authorize the ufe of it. *That* faction *in England* who *moft powerfully oppofed his arbitrary pretenfions.* Macaulay's Hiftory, vol. 3. p. 21: It had better have been *that faction which*, and the fame remark will ferve for the following examples. France, who *was in alliance with Sweden.* Smollett's Voltaire, vol. 6. p. 187. *The* court, who *began t ftudy tle European more nearly than heretofore.* Ib. vol. 9. p. 141. *The cavalry who.* Ib. p. 227.

F   *The*

The cities, who *afpired at liberty.* Ib. vol. 2. p. 32. *That* party *among us,* who *boaft of the higheft regard to liberty, have not poffeffed fufficient liberty of thought in this particular.* Hume's Hiftory, vol. 8. p. 312. *The* family, whom, *at firft, they confider as ufurpers.* Hume's Effays, p. 298. If a perfonification had been intended in thefe cafes, *who* would have been proper ; but in the ftyle of hiftory, there can feldom be a propriety in it, at leaft it cannot be pretended in thefe inftances.

In fome cafes it may be doubtful whether this pronoun be properly applied or not. *The number of fubftantial* inhabitants *with* whom *fome cities abound.* Squire's Anglo-Saxon Government, p. 318. For when a term directly, and neceffarily implies perfons, it certainly may, in many cafes, claim the perfonal relative. *None of the* company, whom *he moft affected, could cure him of the melancholy under which he laboured.* Female American, vol. 1. p. 52. The word *acquaintance,* may have the fame conftruction.

We hardly confider children as perfons, becaufe that term gives us the idea of reafon, and reflection; and therefore, the application of the perfonal relative *who,*

in

in this cafe, feems to be harfh. *A child,
who.* Cadogan.

It is ftill more improperly applied to animals. *A lake, frequented by that* fowl, whom *nature has taught to dip the wing in water.* Raffelas, vol. 1. p. 4.

When the name of a perfon is ufed merely as a name, and does not refer to the perfon; the pronoun *which* ought to be ufed, and not *who. It is no wonder if a man, made up of fuch contrarieties, did not fhine at the court of Queen* Elizabeth, who *was but another name for prudence, and œconomy.*

The word *whofe* begins likewife to be reftricted to perfons, but it is not done fo generally but that good writers, and even in profe, ufe it when fpeaking of things. I do not think, however, that the conftruction is generally pleafing. *Pleafure, whofe nature.* Hume. *Call every* production, whofe *parts exift all at once, and* whofe *nature depends not cn a tranfition for its exiftence, a work or thing done, and not an energy, or operation.* Harris's Hermes. *A true critic in the perufal of a book, is like a* dog *at a feaft;* whofe *thought and ftomach are wholly fet upon what the guefts fling away.* Swift's Tale of a Tub, p. 63.

In one cafe, however, cuſtom authorizes us to uſe *which* with reſpect to perſons ; and that is, when we want to dif-
tinguiſh one perſon of two, or a particular perſon among a number of others.
We ſhould then ſay, *Which of the two, or
which of them, is he or ſhe ?*

That is alſo uſed as a relative, inſtead
of *who* or *which* ; as *the man* that [*for*
whom] *I loved. The houſe* that [*for* which]
I have built. In which caſe it is indeclinable ; as *The men* that *I feared.*

The pronouns *that*, and *who*, or *which*,
may often be uſed promiſcuouſly ; but after an adjective, eſpecially in the ſuperlative degree, *who* or *which* cannot be admitted. *The followers of Catiline were the*
moſt profligate, *which could be called out
of the moſt corrupt city of the univerſe.*
Riſe and Fall of antient Republicks, p.
282. *Lord Henry Sidney was one of the*
wiſeſt, *and* moſt active *governors* whom
Ireland had enjoyed for ſeveral years. Hume's
Hiſtory, vol. 5. p. 415. *The* ableſt *miniſter* whom *James ever poſſeſſed.* Ib. vol.
6. p. 10. *Rumours continually prevailed in
the camp that the adverſe Faction in London were making great Preparations to over-
throw all which had been yielded in favour
of the army.* Macaulay's Hiſtory, vol. 4.
P. 335.

p. 335 This conſtruction, which appears to me very aukward (though not contrary to the rules of any Engliſh grammar) is generally uſed by this writer ; but, in all theſe caſes, *that* ſhould have been uſed.

The pronoun *that* alſo follows *the ſame* more naturally than *who* or *which*. *He is the ſame man that you ſaw before.* But if a prepoſition muſt precede the relative, there is a kind of neceſſity to replace *who* or *which* ; becauſe the pronoun *that* does not admit of ſuch a conſtruction. *Ilis ſubjects looked on his fate with* the ſame *indifference*, to which *they ſaw him totally abandoned.* Hume's Hiſtory, vol. 2. p. 52.

Who is uſed in a very peculiar manner in one familiar phraſe ; as *who ſhall ſay*, i. e. as *if one, or ſome perſon ſhould ſay.*

When, in the firſt of a ſeries of clauſes, the relative *who* has been underſtood, it is aukward to introduce it towards the end of the ſentence. *The Scots, without a head, without union among themſelves, attached, all of them, to different competitors, whoſe title they had, raſhly ſubmitted to the deciſion of this foreign uſurper, and* who *were thereby reduced to an abſolute dependence upon him, could only expect by reſiſtance, to intail upon themſelves and their poſterity, a*

more

more grievous, and destructive servitude.
Hume's History, vol. 2. p. 262.

Whatever relative be used, in one of a
series of clauses, relating to the same antecedent, the same ought to be used in
them all. *It is remarkable, that Holland,*
against which the war was undertaken, and
that, in the very beginning, was reduced to the
brink of destruction, lost nothing. Univerfal History, vol. 25. p. 117. It ought
to have been, *and which in the very begin-*
ning.

III. *Of the Oblique Cases of Pronouns.*

I prefer the term *oblique case* of Dr.
Johnson to *objective case,* which Dr. Lowth
uses. By the old grammarians, the nominative case was called *rectus,* being compared to a line standing upright ; and all
the other cases, being formed by *inflexions,*
or *bending* from it, were called *oblique.*
Now the *objective* case can only stand for
the *accusative,* in which the object of an
affirmative sentence is put ; but *oblique*
comprehends other relations, and other
cases, in which this form of the pronoun
is used ; as, *of me, to me, from me.*

Contrary, as it evidently is, to the analogy of the language, the nominative case
is

is fometimes found after verbs and prepofitions. It has even crept into writing.
*The chaplain intreated my comrade and I to
drefs as well as poffible.* World difplayed,
vol. 1. p. 163. *He told my Lord and I.*
Fair American, vol. 1. p. 141. This
aukward conftruction is conftantly obferved by the author of this romance. On
the other hand, he fometimes ufes the
oblique cafe inftead of the nominative.
My father and him *have been very intimate
fince.* Ib. vol. 2. p. 53. This laft is a
French conftruction.

In one familiar phrafe, the pronoun
me feems to be ufed in the nominative,
and, as it were, in the third perfon too;
but the pronoun and the verb make but
one word. *Methinks already* I *your tears
furvey.* Pope. The word *methought* is
alfo ufed with refpect to time paft; and
even *methoughts.* Female Foundling, vol
1. p. 30.

The nominative cafe is ufed by Shake-
fpeare for the oblique, but it feems to be
in a droll humourous way. *To poor* we
thy enmity is moft capital, i. e. *to us poor
wretches.*

The pronoun *whoever* and *whofoever*
have fometimes a double conftruction, in
imitation of the French idiom. *Elizabeth*

F 4   *pub-*

publickly threatned, that she would have the head of whoever *had advised it.* Hume. *He offered a great recompence to* whomsoever *would help him to a fight of him.* Ib.

The pronoun *whoev r* seems, sometimes, to require two verbs ; and if only one follow, there seems to be a defect in the sentence. *They frequently emit a poisonous juice, whereof* whoever *drinks, that person's brain flies out of his nostrils.* Swift's Tale of a Tub, p. 60.

All our grammarians say, that the nominative cafes of pronouns ought to follow the verb substantive as well as precede it ; yet many familiar forms of speech, and the example of some of our best writers, would lead us to make a contrary rule ; or, at least, would leave us at liberty to adopt which we liked best. *Are these the houses you were speaking of ? Yes, they are* them. *Who is there ? It is* me. *It is* him, *&c. It is not* me *y u are in love with.* Addison. *It cannot be* me. Swift. *To that which once was* thee. Prior. *There is but one man that she can have, and that is* me. Clariffa.

When the word *if* begins a sentence, it seems pretty clear, that no person, whose attention to artificial rules did not put a sensible restraint upon his language, would

ever

ever ufe the nominative cafe after the verb
to be. Who would not fay, *If it be* me,
rather than *If it be* I ?

The word *become* is a verb neuter, as
well as the verb *to be*; and I think that
no perfon, who reads the following fentence will queftion the propriey of the
ufe of the oblique cafe after it. *By imagination we place ourfelves in his fituation,
we conceive ourfelves enduring all the fame
torments, we enter, as it were, into his body,
and become, in fome meafure,* him; *and from
thence form fome idea of his fenfations, and
even feel fomething which, tho' weaker in
degree, is not altogether unlike them.* Smith's
Moral Sentiments, p. 2.

It is, likewife, faid, that the nominative cafe ought to follow the prepofition
than; becaufe the verb *to be* is underftood
after it; As, *You are taller than* he, and
not *taller than him*; becaufe, at full length,
it would be, *You are taller than he is*; but
fince it is allowed, that the oblique cafe
fhould follow prepofitions; and fince the
comparative degree of an adjective, and
the particle *than* have, certainly, betveen
them, the force of a prepofition, expreffing
the relation of one word to another, they
ought to require the oblique cafe of the
pronoun following; fo that *greater than*

F 5   *me,*

me, will be more grammatical than *greater than I*. Examples, however, of this construction, occur in very good writers. *The Jesuits had more interest at court than him.* Smollett's Voltaire, vol. 9. p. 141. *Tell the Cardinal that I understand poetry better than him.* Ib. vol. 8. p. 187. *An inhabitant of Crim Tartary was far more happy than him.* Ib. vol. 6. p. 89.

Perhaps these authorities, and the universal propensity which may be perceived in all persons, as well those who have had a learned and polite education, as those who have not, to these forms of speech, may make it at least doubtful, whether they be not agreeable to the true English idiom. It appears to me, that the chief objection our grammarians have to both these forms, is that they are not agreeable to the idiom of the Latin tongue, which is certainly an argument of little weight, as that language is fundamentally different from ours : whereas those forms of expression are perfectly analogous to the French, and other modern European languages. In these the same form of a pronoun is never used both before and after the verb substantive. Thus the French say, *ce'st moi, ce'st lui* ; and not *c'est je, c'st il.*

Some-

Sometimes, in imitation of the French, the English authors use the oblique case for the nominative. *His wealth and him bid adieu to each other.*

In several cases, as in those abovementioned, the principles of our language are vague, and unsettled. The custom of speaking draws one way; and an attention to arbitrary and artifical rules another. Which will prevail at last, it is impossible to say. It is not the authority of any one person, or of a few, be they ever so eminent, that can establish one form of speech in preference to another. Nothing but the general practice of good writers, and good speakers can do it.

When the pronoun precedes the verb, or the participle by which its case is determined, it is very common, especially in conversation, to use the nominative case where the rules of grammar require the oblique. As, Who *is this* for? Who *should I meet the other day but my old friend.* Spectator, Nº 32. This form of speaking is so familiar, that I question whether grammarians should not admit it as an exception to the general rule. Dr Lowth says, that grammar requires us to say, Whom *do you think me to be.* But in converfation we always hear, Who *do you think me to be.*

Of Verbs.

I. *Of Verbs in general.*

THERE is a peculiar folemnity in the termination *th* of the third perfon fingular of the prefent tenfe of verbs, owing, perhaps, to its being more antient than the termination *s*, which is a corruption of *th*, and which is now become more familiar. *He loveth righteoufnefs, and hateth iniquity. Hath* and *doth* are, for this reafon, more folemn than *has* and *does.*

Some of our later writers, ufe certain neuter verbs, as if they were tranfitive, putting after them the oblique cafe of the pronoun, which was the nominative cafe to it, agreeable to the French conftruction of reciprocal verbs; but this cuftom is fo foreign to the idiom of the Englifh tongue, that I think it can never take generally. *Repenting him of his defign.* Hume's Hiftory, vol. 2. p. 56. *The king foon found reafon to* repent him *of his provoking*
fuch

fuch dangerous enemies. Ib. vol. 1. p. 121.
The popular lords did not fail to enlarge
themfelves *on the fubject.* Macaulay's Hiftory, vol. 3. p. 177. *The nearer his military
fucceffes* approached him *to the throne.*
Hume's Hiftory, vol. 5. p. 383.

In the following fentences, on the contrary, there is a want of the reciprocal
form, a verb active and tranfitive being
ufed as a verb neuter. *Providence gives
us notice, by fenfible declenfions, that we may
difengage from the world by degrees.* Col-
lier. i. e. *difengage ourfelves.*

On the other hand, verbs neuter are
often ufed as if they were active and
tranfitive, without being ufed in a reciprocal conftruction. *Henry knew, that an
excommunication could not fail of* operating
the moft dangerous effects. Hume's Hift.
vol. 2. p. 165. Bargaining *their prince
for money.* Ib. vol. 7. p. 80. *With a view
of* enterprifing *fome new violence.* Ib. p.
387. *All caufes, with regard to the reve-
nue, are* appealed *ultimately to the magiftrates.* Hume's Political Effays, p. 258.
A parliament forfeited *all thofe who had
borne arms againft the king.* Hume's Hift.
vol. 2. p. 223. *The practice of* forfeiting
fhips which had been wrecked. Ib. vol. 1.
p. 500.

We

We have one word, which is ufed as a verb in one fingle conftruction, but which is very unlike a verb in other refpects ; *I had as lief fay a thing after him as after another.* Lowth's Anfwer to Warburton. i. e. *I fhould as foon chufe to fay.* This is a colloquial and familiar phrafe, and is not often found in writing. We have feveral other remarkable contractions for verbs and fentences. *Good, my Lord, confider with yourfelf, the difficulty of this fcience.* Law Tracts, vol. 1. p. 121. i. e. *I beg of you, my Lord.* The phrafe is not common, and low.

There is fomething very fingular in the ufe and conftruction of the verb *ail.* We fay, *what ails him, he ails fomething,* or *he ails nothing* ; but not, *he ails a fever,* or *a fever ails him.*

It is remarkable, that we have one fingle inftance of a proper imperative mood, in the firft perfon plural ; but I believe it is not known except in the Yorkfhire dialect. It is *gâ,* which fignifies, *let us go, eamus.*

The old verb *behoved* is generally ufed imperfonally, with the pronoun *it* preceding it ; but fome perfons affect to give it a proper nominative cafe. *In order to reach our globe* they [the genii] behoved *to have wings.* Smollett's Voltaire, vol. 16. p. 156. that is, *it behoved them to have wings.* But as *this signal revolution in* the criminal law behoved *to be galling to individuals, unaccuftomed to reftrain their paffions, all meafures were taken to make the yoke eafy.* Law Tracts, vol. 1. p. 96, that is, *were neceffarily galling,* or *could not but be galling.* I think this conftruction, which is by no means Englifh, is peculiar to Scotland.

The verb *irks* is only ufed imperfonally; as, *it irks me,* which is nearly equivalent to *it grieves me.*

In fome very familiar forms of fpeech, the active feems to be put for the paffive form of verbs and participles. *I'll teach you all what's* owing *to your Queen.* Dryden. *The books continue felling,* i. e. *upon the fale,* or *to be fold.* It may be fuppofed, that this inftance is a contracted form of fpeaking, the word ending in *ing,* being a noun, and the prepofition being underftood; fo we fay, *the brafs is forging,* i. e. *at the forging,* or *in the act of forging.* But the following fentences are not fo eafily explained; *They are to blame,* i. e. *to be blamed. The books are to bind,* i. e. *to be bound.* In the phrafe, *he may be ftill to feek for a thing,* the fenfe feems to require, that

that the ellipſis be ſupplied by reading. *he may ſtill be in a condition to ſeek it,* or *in a ſtate of ſeeking it,* i. e. *he may not yet have found what he was ſeeking.*

In ſome familiar phraſes, the ſubject and object of an affirmation ſeem to be tranſpoſed. We ſay, He is *well* read *in hiſtory,* when we mean that hiſtory is well read by him. They were aſked *a queſtion,* i. e. *a queſtion was aſked them.* They were offered *twenty ſhillings,* i. e. *twenty ſhillings were offered them. They were offered a pardon,* i. e. *a pardon was offered to them.* This inverſion of the nominative caſe, as it may be called, may ſometimes make a perſon pauſe, a little, before he finds the true ſenſe of a paſſage. *During his reſidence abroad,* he *had acquired immenſe riches, and* had been left, *by a friend, no leſs than eighty thouſand pounds, to take the name of Melmoth.* Louiſa Mildmay, vol. 2. p. 222.

When verbs end in *s, ſe, ſs, k, p,* and ſome other letters, the preter tenſe, and participles, in the manner in which we generally pronounce words in Engliſh, end as if the final letter was *t*; but it does not look well to make any abridgment in writing, and much leſs to ſpell the word with a *t.* Theſe contractions, however, have often been made by good writers.

Diſperſt.

VERBS.

Disperst. Hume's History, vol. 3. p. 390.
Distrest. Ib. vol. 2. p. 224. *Dropt.* Ib.
vol. 4. p 408. *Talkt.* Hume's Essays,
p. 295. *Checkt.* Ib. p. 297. *Askt.* Ib.
p. 305. *His face* stampt *upon their coins.*
Addison. Enwrapt *in those studies.* Pope,
and Arbuthnot. *He* past *four months.*
Rasselas, vol. 1. p. 28. Heapt *up greater
honours.* Addison. In verse, this contraction is more allowable; Rapt *into future times, the bard begun.* Pope's Mef-
fiah.

The verb *ought* is not enumerated
among the auxiliary verbs, becaufe it
does not connect with the other verbs,
without the intervention of the particle *to.*
It is an imperfect verb, for it has no other
modification befides this one.

The verb *must*, which was enumerated
among the auxiliaries, is equally imperfect, and is likewife of the prefent tenfe
only. It is, therefore, improperly introduced into a fentence which relates wholly
to time paft. Muft *it not be expected, that
the king would defend an authority, which
had been exercifed without difpute or contro-
verfy.* Hume's Hiftory, vol. 8. p. 311.
The meaning is, *might it not have been expected.*

The

The prefent tenfe is improperly ufed with refpect to a time, which is mentioned as having a certain limited duration ; becaufe the time mult be paft or future. *I have compaffion on the multitude becaufe* they continue *with me, now,* three days. It fhould have been, *have continued.* Indeed the verb *have* is appropriated to this very ufe. *In the treafury belonging to the cathedral in this city* is preferved *with the greateft veneration, for* upwards of fix hundred years, *a d fh, or rather an hexagon bowl, which they pretend to be made of emerald.* Condamine's Travels, p. 15. *It is at Rome, that* it is cultivated *with the greateft fuccefs, and efpecially for* upwards of a century paft. Ib. p. 43. *I remember him thefe many years.* Englifh Merchant.

An ambiguity is occafioned in our language when the preter tenfe of one verb happens to be the prefent tenfe of another. I fell *a tree now.* I fell *down yefterday,* from the verb *to fall. I* lay *a thing down to day: I* lay *down yefterday,* from the verb *to lie*

The termination *eft,* annexed to the preter tenfes of verbs, is, at beft, a very harfh one, when it is contracted, according to our general cuftom, by throwing out the *e* ; as *learnedft,* for *learnedeft* ; and efpecially,

efpecially, if it be again contracted into
one fyllable, as it is commonly pronounced, and made *learndft*. Some forms of
the preter tenfes, where they are always
contracted in the firft perfon, do not admit of any more contraction, or the addition of any more confonants to their terminations; and therefore may be properly
enough faid to have no fecond perfons
fingular at all. I believe a writer, or
fpeaker would have recourfe to any periphrafis rather than fay *kepteft*, or *keptft*,
which are the only words that can be fuppofed to be the fecond perfons in the
tenfe *I kept*. Or, in what manner would
the termination of the fecond perfon be
annexed to the word *dreamed*, or, as it is
generally pronounced, *dreamt*. Indeed
this harfh termination *eft* is generally
quite dropped in common converfation,
and fometimes by the poets, in writing.
Nor thou that flings (for *flingeft*, or *flingft*)
me floundring from thy back. Frogs and
Mice, line 123.

II. *Of*

II. *Of the Conjunctive Form of Verbs.*

The word *had* is frequently used instead of *would have,* in which case it has
all the force of a conjunctive form of a
verb. *He* had *been Diogenes if he had not
been Alexander,* i. e. *would have been, &c.*
The verb *had* in this sense precedes its
nominative case, and the particle implying doubt or uncertainty is omitted. *Had
he done this, he would have escaped;* i. e.
*if he had done this. No landholder would
have been at that expence,* had he *not been
sure of the sale of his commodities.* Postle-
thwaite on Commerce, p. 123.

There seems to be a peculiar elegance
in a sentence beginning with the conjunctive form of a verb. *Were there no difference, there would be no choice.* Harris's
three Treatises, p. 208.

A double conjunctive, in two corres-
ponding clauses of a sentence, is still
more elegant. *He* had *formed one of the
most shining characters of his age,* had *not
the extreme narrowness of his genius, in every
thing but war, diminished the lustre of his
merits.* Hume's History, vol. 7. p. 28.
The sentence in the common form,
would not have read near so well. *He*
would

would have formed, &c. *if the extreme nar-
rowne/s of his genius,* &c. *had not,* &c.
Had *the limitations on the prerogative been,
in his time, quite fixed, and certain, his integrity* had *made him regard as /acred, the
boundaries of the conftitution.* Ib. p. 151.

Sometimes the particles expreffing fuppofition are omitted before the conjunctive
form of verbs, this form itfelf fufficiently
expreffing uncertainty.   Were *tho/e letters
to fall into the hands of /ome ingenious per/ons.*
Bolingbroke on Hiftory, vol. 1. p. 5. i. e.
If the/e letters were to fall, &c.

The conjunctive form may take place
after the adverb *perhaps.   Perhaps it were
to be wi/hed, that, in bani/hing from the
pulpit that /al/e ta/te, whereby it had been
/o long deba/ed, he had al/o /uppre//ed the
cu/tom of preaching from one text.* Smollett's Voltaire, vol. 9. p. 5.

Mr. *John/on* affigns no conjunctive form
to the *preter ten/e:* but the analogy of
the language feems to require that both
the tenfes be put upon a level in this refpect.—It feems to be ufed with propriety
only when fome degree of *doubt* or *he/ita-
tion* is implied; fince when an event is
looked upon as abfolutely certain, though
in fpeaking of it we make ufe of the conjunctive particles, *&c.* the ufual change
of

of terminations is retained : to give a familiar example of this ; we fhould fay, in purfuing a perfon, *We fhould overtake him though* he run ; not knowing whether he did run or no ; whereas, upon feeing him run, we fhould fay, *We fhall overtake him though* he runneth, or *runs.*

Almoft all the irregularities in the conftruction of any language arife from the *ellipfis* of fome words which were originally inferted in the fentence, and made it regular : let us endeavour to explain this manner of fpeaking, by tracing out the original ellipfis. May we not fuppofe that the word *run* in this fentence is in the *radical form* (which anfwers to the *infinitive mood* in other languages) requiring regularly to be preceded by another verb expreffing doubt or uncertainty, and the intire fentence to be, *We fhall overtake him though he* fhould *run.*

It is an objection, however, to this account of the origin of the conjunctive form of verbs, at leaft, an objection againft extending it to the preter tenfe ; that, if we analize a conjunctive preterite, by fupplying the ellipfis, the rule will not appear to hold, except when the preter tenfe and the participle are the fame, as indeed they are in all verbs regularly inflected.

inflected. *If thou loved,* may be rendered, *If thou shouldest have loved,* or *If thou hadst loved* ; but *if thou drew,* would be, *If thou hadst drawn.*

That the conjunctive form of verbs is, however, in fact ufed for the auxiliary and another form of the verb, is evident from a variety of examples. *What a school of private and public virtue* had been *opened to us, after the refurrection of letters, if the late historians of the Roman commonwealth, and the first of the succeeding monarchy, had come down to us entire. Would have been opened* makes exactly the fame fenfe. *Many acts, which* had been *blameable in a peaceable government, were employed to detect confpiracies.* Hume's Hiftory, vol. 5. p. 261. i. e. *would have been blameable.*

Thefe examples are exactly fimilar to the following, which is, undeniably, in what I call the conjunctive form. *They affirmed, that* it were *injuftice to deny the execution of the law to any individual,* i. e. that it would be injuftice, &c.

This conjunctive form of verbs, though our forefathers paid a pretty ftrict regard to it, is much neglected by many of our beft writers. *If he* chances *to think right, he knows not how to convey his thoughts to another,*

another, with clearnefs and perfpicuity. Addifon.

So little is this form of verbs attended to, that few writers are quite uniform in their own practice with refpect to it. We even, fometimes, find both the forms of a verb in the fame fentence, and in the fame conftruction. *If a man* prefer *a life of induftry, it is becaufe he has an idea of happinefs in wealth ; if he* prefers *a life of gaiety, it is from a like idea concerning pleafure.* Harris's three Treatifes, p. 124. *No reafonable man, whether whig or tory, can be of opinion for continuing the war, upon the foot it now is, unlefs he* be *a gainer by it, and* hopes, *it may occafion fome new turn of affairs at home, to the advantage of his party ; or unlefs he* be *very ignorant of the kingdom's condition, and by what means we have been reduced to it.* Swift's Preface, to the Conduct of the Allies.

Grammatical as this conjunctive form of verbs is faid to be, by all who write upon the fubject, it muft, I think, be acknowledged, that it fometimes gives the appearance of ftiffnefs, and harfhnefs to a fentence. *That no pretenfions to fo illuftrious a character, fhould by any means be received before that operation were performed.* Swift's Tale of a Tub, p. 55.

† *We*

We fhould owe little to that ftatefman, who were to contrive a defence, that might fuper-fede the external ufe of virtue. Fergufon's Hiftory of Civil Society, p. 92.

Originally, the two forms of the verb *to be* were ufed promifcuoufly. *We be twelve brethren.* Genefis.

III. *Of Participles.*

To avoid a collifion of vowels, the *e* is omitted before *i* in participles of the prefent tenfe; as, *love, loving.* On the other hand, the final confonant is doubled in the fame cafe; and indeed before any other addition to the termination, when it is preceded by a fingle vowel, and when, if it confift of two fyllables, the accent would be upon the latter of them; as, *get, getting, getteth; forget, forgetting, for-getteth.*

Many participles, lofing the idea of time, which was originally annexed to them, become, in all refpects, mere adjectives; as, *charming youth, a loving couple. A regular formed fervitude.* Hume's Hiftory, vol. 7. p. 105. *A formed defign to fubvert the conftitution.* Ib. vol. 6. p. 285. *A fettled defign.* Ib. vol. 7. p. 86. *A well appointed army.* Ib. vol. 7. p. 466.

G   There

There is great elegance in fome of thefe adjectives, made out of participles.

In this cafe, the termination *ed* is commonly contracted, and the words are made to end in *t*; as, *time paft*, from *paffed*. Sometimes the termination *ed* is dropped entirely, when the verb itfelf ended in *t*, and when the words have wholly loft their original ufe. as participles ; as, *content*, *correct*, *corrupt*, &c.

Many nouns are derived from verbs, and end in *ing*, like participles of the prefent tenfe. The difference between thefe nouns and participles is often overlooked, and the accurate diftinction of the two fenfes not attended to. If I fay, *What think you of my* horfe's running *to-day*, I ufe the noun *running*, and fuppofe the horfe to have actually run; for it is the fame thing as if I had faid, *What think you of the running of my horfe.* But if I fay, *What think you of my* horfe running *to-day*, I ufe the participle, and I mean to afk, whether it be proper that my horfe fhould run or not ; which, therefore, fuppofes that he had not then run.

Some of our early poets preferve the *y*, as the remains of the Saxon *ge*, prefixed to many participles. Thus Spencer writes, *ypight* for *pitched*.

Some

Some of our participles feem to have been more irregular formerly than they are now; as, befides the example above-mentioned, Spencer writes *fhright* for *fhrieked.*

Formerly the *d*, which terminates participles preterite, was often dropped, when the verb ended in *e*. *They are* confederate *againft thee.* Pfalms. This form of the participle is ftill common among the Scots. *They engaged the bifhops to pronounce Ga- rifton* excommunicate, *if he remained any longer in the kingdom.* Hume's Hiftory, vol. 2. p. 341 The word *fituate* is often ufed, and efpecially by lawyers, for *fitu ated.* Milton fometimes ufes this form, as *elevate* for *elevated.*

As the *paucity of inflections* is the greateft defect in our language, we ought to take advantage of every variety that the practice of good authors will warrant ; and, therefore, if poffible, make a *participle* different from the *preterite* of a verb ; as, a book is *written*, not *wrote* ; the fhips are *taken*, not *took.*

This rule, however, has, by no means, been fufficiently attended to by good writers. *It was not* wrote *on parchment.* Hume's Effays, p. 262. *The court of Au- guftus has not yet* wore *off the manners of*
the

the republick. Ib. p. 182. *You who have* forfook *them.* Smollett's Voltaire, vol. 18. p. 27. *Who have* bore *a part in the progrefs.* Fergufon on Civil Society, p. 261.

In fome cafes, the cuftom of leaving out the *n,* in the termination of participles, hath prevailed fo long, that it feems too late to attempt to reftore it. Thus the word *broke* feems almoft to have excluded *broken.* *Whenever a ftanding rule of law hath been wantonly* broke *in upon.* Blackftone's Commentaries, vol. 1. p. 70. *Their line of princes was continually* broke. Hume's Effays, ɔ 502.

Bolingbroke affects a difference in fpelling the preter tenfes and participles of verbs, when they are the fame in found with the prefent tenfe. *The late Duke of Marlborough never* red *Xenophon, moft certainly* Bolingbroke on Hiftory, vol. 1. p. 26. *I remember to have* red. Ib. p. 68. This inftance is particularly bad, on account of the adjective being likewife fpelled *red.* *Wherever chriftianity has* fpred. Ib. p. 92. Mr. Hume fpells the preterite in the fame manner. *Such illuftrious examples* fpred *knowledge every where, and begat an univerfal efteem for the fciences.* Hume's Effays, p. 282.

Boling-

Bolingbroke, in one place, feems to affect a variety in the participles of the fame verb, when they happen to come too near together. *He will endeavour to write as the antient author would have* wrote, *had he* writ *in the fame language.* Bolingbroke on Hiftory, vol. 1. p. 68.

The affectation of ufing the preterite tenfe inftead of the participle, which is common, I think, in the dialect of London, is peculiarly aukward ; as, *he has* came. This has fometimes crept into writing. *If fome events had not* fell *out.* Poftlethwaite on Commerce, Pref. p. 11.

Different participles of the fame verb are fometimes ufed in different fenfes. Thus we fay, *a man is* hanged ; but, *the coat is* hung up.

There is a remarkable ambiguity in the ufe of the participle preterite, as the fame word may exprefs a thing either doing, or done. *I went to fee the child* dreffed, may either mean, I went to fee the child whilft they were putting on its cloaths, or when they were put on.

IV. *Of the Auxiliary Verbs.*

It is often unneceſſary to repeat the principal verb after an auxiliary, when it has been uſed before in the ſame ſentence, and the ſame conſtruction. *I have read that auther, but* you have *not. He loves net plays, as* thou doſt, *Anthony.* Shakeſpeare.

By ſtudying conciſeneſs we are apt to drop the auxiliary *to have,* though the ſenſe relate to the time paſt. *I found him better than I expected to find him.* In this caſe, analogy ſeems to require that we ſay, *then I expected to have found him.* i. e. *to have found him* then. On the other hand, as the time paſt is ſufficiently indicated in the former part of the ſentence, and *to find* may be ſaid to be indefinite with reſpect to time, the repetition of the auxiliary will perhaps, by ſome, be thought aukward, and unneceſſary.

In many caſes, however, writers are certainly faulty in omitting this auxiliary. *Theſe proſecutions of William,* ſeem to be *the moſt iniquitous meaſures purſued by the court, during the time that the uſe of parliaments was ſuſpended.* Hume's Hiſtory, vol. 6. p. 248. *To have been,* is what the ſenſe

of

of this paſſage requires. *The following converſation is, in its kind, ſomewhat uncommon; and, for this reaſon, I have remembered it more minutely than* I could jmagine. Harris. i. e. *I could have imagined.*

Notwithſtanding this, when the word *have* occurs more than once in a ſentence, it ſeems to embarraſs it, and one of them ſeems to be ſuperfluous; though, both of them being uſed in the ſame conſtruction, and relating to the ſame time, there ſeems to be an equal propriety in them both. The following ſentences do not, on this account, read well, though they may be ſtrictly grammatical: *Hiſtory painters would have found it difficult, to have invented ſuch a ſpecies of beings, when they were obliged to put a moral virtue into colours.* Addiſon on Medals. *The girl ſaid, if her maſter would but have let her had morey, to have ſent for proper advice, and broths, and jellies, and ſuch like, ſhe might have been well long ago.* George Villiers, vol. 2. p. 90.

It ſeems not to have been determined by the Engliſh grammarians, whether the paſſive participles of verbs neuter require the auxiliary *am* or *have* before them: The French, in this caſe, confine themſelves ſtrictly to the former. *If ſuch maxims, and ſuch practices prevail, what* has

become

become *of national liberty.* Hume's Hiftory, vol. 6. p. 254. The French would fay, *what is become*; and in this inftance, perhaps, with more propriety. Yet I think we have an advantage in the choice of thefe two forms of expreffion, as it appears to me, that we ufe them to exprefs different modifications of the fenfe. When I fay, *I am fallen*, I mean at this prefent inftant; whereas, if I fay, *I have fallen*, my meaning comprehends, indeed, the foregoing; but has, likewife, a fecret reference to fome period of time paft, as *fome time in this day*, or *in this hour*, *I have fallen*; implying fome continuance of time, which the other form of expreffion does not.

The conditional form of the verbs *fhall*, &c. is ufed with refpect to time paft, prefent, and future. We fay, *I fhould have gone yefterday*, and *I fhould go to-day*, or *tomorrow*; but the abfolute form *I fhall*, always refpects time to come.

Sometimes that form of the auxiliary verbs *fhall*, *will*, *may*, and *can*, which is generally conditional, is elegantly ufed to exprefs a very flight affertion, with a modeft diffidence. Thus we fay, *I fhould think*; that is, *I am rather inclined to think*. *The general report is*, *that* he fhould have

said

said *in confidence to Clifford, that if he was
sure the young man who appeared in Flanders
was really son to king Edward, he never
would bear arms against him.* Hume's Hiftory, vol. 3. p. 383. *The royal power, it
should seem, might be intrufted in their hands.*
Ib. vol. 6. p. 217.

The auxiliary verb *shall* reverts to its
original fignification in its conditional
form, when *if*, or any other particle expreffing uncertainty, is prefixed to it. *I
should go*, means I ought to go ; but *if I
should go*, means *if it happen that I go.*
This obfervation is Mr. Johnfon's.

This conditional form of thefe verbs,
at the beginning of a fentence, has often
the force of a ftrong wifh, or imprecation.
In this fenfe it is generally found in conjunction with the word *to*. Would to
heaven, *young man, I knew you.* Fair
American, vol. 1. p. 28. that is, *by heaven,
I wish I knew you.*   But fometimes we find
it without the particle *to*. *Mine Eyes are
open now* ; would, *Zepir, thine wers too.*
Smollett's Voltaire, vol. 25. .p. 35.
Would, *that kind heaven had ta'en my
wretched life.* Ib. vol. 28. p. 49.

The Scots ftill ufe *shall* and *will*, *should*
and *would*, as they were formerly ufed in
England ; i. e. in a fenfe quite contrary

to

to that in which they are ufed with us at prefent. *We* would *have been wanting to ourfelves, if we did continue to pay a fubfidy, for which there was no neceffity.* Conduct of the Whigs and Tories examined. *We* will, *therefore, briefly unfold the reafons which induce us to believe, that this nation really enjoyed a confiderable trade before this aufpicious reign. We* will *next fhow what thofe difficulties were, under which our commerce laboured under the reign preceding that*; *and, laftly, we* will *give a fhort account how thofe advantages arofe, of which we have been fince poffeffed.* Preceptor, vol. 2. p. 413. *By fuch gradual innovations the king flattered himfelf that he* would *quietly introduce epifcopal authority.* Hume's Hiftory, vol. 6. p. 22. *He imagined, that by playing one party againft the other, he* would *eafily obtain the victory over both,* Ib. vol. 8. p. 250.

In feveral familiar forms of expreffion, the word *fhall* ftill retains its original fignification, and does not mean to promife, threaten, or engage, in the third perfon, but the mere futurition of an event ; as, *This is as extraordinary a thing as one* fhall *ever hear of.* This fenfe is alfo retained by our beft writers in the graveft ftyle. *Whoever* will *examine the writirgs of all kinds,*

*kinds, wherewith this antient sect hath ho-
noured the world,* ſhall *immediately find, from
the whole thread and tenor of them, that the
ideas of the authors have been altogether
converſant, and taken up with the faults,
and blemiſhes, and overſights, and miſtakes
of other writers.* Swift. It ſhould ſeem
that both the words *ſhall* and *will* might
be ſubſtituted for one another in this paſſage, without any injury to the ſenſe.
*Put this reverſe now, if you pleaſe, into
the hands of a muſical antiquary,* he ſhall
*tell you, that the uſe of the ſhield, being to
defend the body from the weapons of an enemy, it very aptly ſhadows out to us the reſo-
lution, or continence of the Emperor.* Addiſon on Medals, p. 31.

When a queſtion is aſked, the verb
ſhall, in the firſt perſon, is uſed in a ſenſe
different from both its other ſenſes. *Shall
I write,* means, *Is it your pleaſure that I
ſhould write. Will,* in the ſecond perſon,
only reverts to its other uſual ſenſe ; for,
Will you write, means, *Is it your intention
to write.*

When the word *will* is no auxiliary,
but is uſed by itſelf, to expreſs volition,
it is inflected regularly, like other verbs.
*Nor is the ſubtle air leſs obedient to thy pow-
or, whether thou* willeſt *it to be a miniſter*

to our pleasure, or utility. Harris's three Treatises, p. 39.

In asking a question, the auxiliary verb *may* is sometimes used without any regard to its general meaning, but only, as it were, to soften the boldness there might be in an inquiry; as, *How old may you be,* &c.

When the preposition *to* signifies *in order to,* it used to be preceded by *for,* which is now almost obsolete; *What went you out for to see.* This exactly corresponds to the use which the French make of *pour.*

The particle *for* before the infinitive, is not, in all cases, obsolete. It is used if the subject of the affirmation intervene between that preposition and the verb. For *holy persons* to be *humble, is as hard, as* for *a prince to submit himself* to be *guided by tutors.* Taylor.

The verb *dare* is sometimes used without the preposition *to* after it, as if it was an auxiliary verb. *Who* durst defy *the omnipotent to arms.* Milton. *Who have* dared defy *the worst.* Harris's three Treatises, p. 200. *I dare swear you think my letter already long enough.* Lady Montague's Letters, vol. 1. p. 6. *I had a good deal of courage to* dare mount *him.*

This conftruction, however, does not feem natural, except in fuch familiar expreffions as *I dare fay, I dare go*, and the like. It muft, I fuppofe, be according to the Scotch idiom, that Mrs. Macaulay omits it after the verb *help. Laud was promoted as an ufeful inftrument, to* help carry *on the new meafures of the court.* Hiftory, vol. 4. p. 150.

SECTION VI.

Of Adverbs and Conjunctions.

MANY adverbs admit of degrees of comparifon as well as adjectives, and for the fame reafon ; as, *foon, fooner, fooneft; well, better, beft; often, oftener, ofteneft.*

In imitation of the French idiom, the adverb of place *where* is often ufed inftead of the pronoun relative, and a prepofition. *They framed a proteftation*, where *they repeated all their former claims.* Hume's Hiftory. i. e. in which *they repeated. The king was ftill determined to run forwards in the fame courfe* where *he was already, by his*

preci-

precipitate career, too fatally advanced.
Ib. i. e. in which *he was.*

The adverbs *hence, thence,* and *whence,* imply a prepofition; for they fignify, *from this place, from that place, from what place.* It feems, therefore, to be improper to join a prepofition along with them, becaufe it is fuperfluous ; yet the practice is very common. *This is the leviathan,* from whence *the terrible wits of our age are faid to borrow their weapons.* Swift's Tale of a Tub, p. 10. *An ancient author prophecies* from hence. Dryden. Indeed the origin of thefe words is fo little attended to, and the prepofition *from* fo often ufed in conftruction with them, that the omiffion of it in many cafes would feem ftiff and difagreeable.

We have fome examples of adverbs being ufed for fubftantives. *In* 1687 *Innocent the eleventh erected it into a community of regulars, fince* when *it has begun to increafe in thofe countries as a religious order.* Ulloa's Voyage, vol. 1. p. 270. i. e. *fince which time.* A little while, *and I fhall not fee you,* i. e. *a fhort time.* It is worth their while, i. e. *it deferves their time and pains.* But this ufe of the word rather fuits familiar and low ftyle. The fame may be faid of the phrafe, *to do a thing* any how,

i. e.

i. e. *in any manner*; or, *some how*, i. e. *in some manner.* Somehow, *worthy as these people are, they look upon public penance as disreputable.* Louisa Mildmay, vol. 2. p. 175.

The adverb *how* is sometimes used in a particular sense, implying a negative. *Let us take care* how *we sin,* i. e. *Let us take care that we do not sin.* The same construction has not, however, always the same sense. *Take care* how *ye hear,* i. e. *in what manner ye hear.*

Sometimes this adverb *how* is equivalent to the conjunction *that. It has been matter of astonishment to me,* how *such persons could take so many silly pains to establish mystery on metaphysics.* Bolingbroke on History, vol. 1. p. 175. i. e. *that such persons——*

Adverbs are more often put for adjectives, agreeably to the idiom of the Greek tongue. *The action was* amiss, *the* then *ministry.* Conduct of the Whigs and Tories examined. *The idea is* alike *in both.* Addison on Medals, p. 70. *The above* discourse. Harris's three Treatises, p. 95.

One use of the adverb *there* is pretty remarkable, though common. It is prefixed to a verb, when the nominative case follows it; but seems to have no meaning what-

whatever, except it be thought to give a
fmall degree of emphafis to the fentence.
There was *a man fent from God, whofe
name was John*; i. e. a man was fent.

In fome cafes, two negative particles
were formerly ufed, as in Greek, where
we now ufe only one. *And this fterre,
which is toward the northe, that we clippen
the lode fterre,* ne *appeareth* not *to hem.*
Maundeville.

When the negative is included in the
fubject of an affirmation, a negative meaning has the appearance of a pofitive one.
I can do nothing, i. e. *I cannot do any thing.*

The words *no* and *not* are ufed varioufly
by our beft writers, and fometimes even
promifcuoufly by the fame writer. *Whether
it be fo or no.* Addifon. *Hence ; whether, in imitation of Catullus, or not, we
apply the fame thought to the moon.* Ib.

There is a remarkable ambiguity in the
ufe of the negative adjective *no* ; and I
do not fee how it can be remedied in any
language. If I fay, *no laws are better
than the Englifh,* it is only my known fentiments that can inform a perfon whether
I mean to praife, or difpraife them.

It is obfervable, that an anfwer to a
queftion, in Englifh, is rather a contraction
of a fentence, expreffing an affirmative or
negative propofition, and that it does not

at

at all depend on the manner in which the queſtion is aſked. Whether my friend ſay, Are you *diſpoſed to take a walk* ; or, Are you not *diſpoſed to take a walk* ; if I be diſpoſed to walk, I ſay, *yes* ; if not, I ſay, *no.*

The word *ſo* has, ſometimes, the ſame meaning with *alſo, likewiſe, the ſame* ; or rather it is equivalent to the univerſal pronoun *le* in French. *They are happy, we are not* ſo, i. e. *not happy.*

Mr. Hume frequently enumerates a great number of particulars without any conjunction whatever between any of them. This conſtruction, though it very happily expreſſes rapidity and energy, ſeems to have a bad effect in plain hiſtorical ſtyle, as it makes a diſagreeable *hiatus*, and diſappoints the reader. *They enacted, that no proclamation ſhould deprive any perſon of his lawful poſſeſſions, liberties, inheritances, privileges, franchiſes ; nor yet infringe any common law, or laudable cuſtom of the realm.* Hume's Hiſtory, vol. 4. p. 214. *They were commanded by Deſſé, and under him by Andelet, Strozzi, Miellrage, Count Rhingrave.* This conſtruction, where great numbers of proper names occur, is very common with this author.

Some-

Sometimes the particles *or*, and *nor*, may, either of them, be ufed with nearly equal propriety. *The king, whofe character was not fufficiently vigorous, nor decifive, affented to the meafure.* Hume's Hiftory, vol. 6. p. 102. *Or* would perhaps have been better, but *nor* feems to repeat the nega- tion in the former part of the fentence, and therefore gives more emphafis to the expreffion.

The conjunction *as* is feldom ufed but in connection with fome other conjunc- tion, or in dependance upon fome other word of the fentence; but, in one cafe, it is ufed fingly, in the fame fenfe as the prepofition *in*. *The books were to have been fold, as this day.*

That is ufed improperly in the follow- ing fentences, in which the French and not the Englifh idiom is obferved. *The refo- lution was not the lefs fixed, that the fecret was as yet communicated to very few, either in the French or the Englifh court.* Hume's Hiftory, vol. 7. p. 474. *We will not pre- tend to examine difeafes in all their various circumftances, efpecially that they have not been fo accurately obferved or defcribed by writers of later ages, as were to be wifhed.* Martine's Effays, p. 29. *Though nothing urged by the kings friends on this occafion had*
any

any connection with the peace, security, and freedom the Scots at this time enjoyed; and that *their proposal of engaging against England manifestly tended to the utter destruction of these bl ssings; yet the forem.ntioned arguments had such weight with the parliament, that a committee of twenty-four members was empowered to provide for the safety of the kingdom.* Macaulay's Hist. vol. 4. p. 377.

In several cases we content ourselves, now, with fewer conjunctive particles than our ancestors did; particularly, we often leave out the conjunction *as,* when they used it, after *so*; and the use of it in those cases now appears aukward. *This new associate proposed abundance of theses against indulgences,* so as that *his doctrines were embraced by great numbers.* Universal Hist. vol. 29. p. 501. *So that* would have been much easier, and better.

We want a conjunction adapted to familiar style, equivalent to *notwithstanding. For all that* seems to be too low and vulgar. *A word it was in the mouth of every one,* but for all that, *as to its precise and definite idea, this may still be a secret.* Harris's three Treatises, p. 5.

In regard that is solemn, and antiquated; *because* would do much better in the following sentence. *The French musick is disliked*

liked by all other nations. It cannot be other-wise, in regard that *the French profody dif-fers from that of every other country in Europe.* Smollett's Voltaire, vol. 9. p. 306.

Except is far preferable to *other than. It admitted of no effectual cure,* other than *amputation.* Law Tracts, vol. 1. p. 302. and alfo to *all but. They arofe in the morning, and lay down at night, pleafed with each other, and themfelves,* all but *Raffelas, who began to withdraw himfelf from their paftime.* Raffelas, vol. 1. p. 11.

SECTION VII.

Of the Compofition and Derivation of Words.

WHEN two words are ufed to com-pofe one, in order to make one name of a thing, they often coalefce into one word, and are written clofe together; as *glafshoufe, countryman.* Sometimes an ſ is interpofed between them, the for-mer having been a genitive cafe; as, *Herdfman*; originally, *Herd's man.* In other cafes, though the idea be one, the words

words remain quite separate, as *country gentleman, grammar school, Pendervin castle, city gates,* &c. Other terms remain in a kind of middle state; and the two word, not perfectly coalescing into one, are usually joined by a hyphen; as, *court-day, court-hand, knight-errant, crofs-bar-fhot*; but these hyphens are now generally omitted. They are most used to connect some Latin particle to a word; as *non-conductor, non-electric.* It is also sometimes used after the prefixes *re* and *pre,* when they are joined to words beginning with an *e,* as, *re-enter, pre-eminence,* &c. The hyphen is also sometimes used to connect particles to other words, in order to compound the idea; an *unheard-of reftraint.* Hume's Hiftory, vol. 7. p. 449. *Counterproject.* Swift. Words of this kind are eafily underftood, becaufe their meaning out of compofition is retained when they are compounded. *All-conqueror as I am.* Smollett's Voltaire, vol. 27. p. 292.

For want of a fufficient number of terms to exprefs the afcending and defcending lines of confanguinity, we aukwardly repeat the word *great* for every generation above grandfather, and below grandfon, as *great great grandfather, great great grandfon,* &c.

Prepo-

Prepofitions are often joined to adverbs, fo as to make one word with them ; as *hereabouts, hereafter, herein,* &c. but thefe words are now feldom ufed, except in formal and folemn ftyle.

, A very great number of the moft common and fignificant phrafes in our language are made by the addition of a prepofition to a verb, particularly the Saxon monofyllabic verbs, as *to get, to keep, to make, to give, to caft, to go, to hold,* &c. In the cafe of thefe complex terms, the component parts are no guide to the fenfe of the whole. Thus the common idea annexed to the verb *give* is loft in the phrafes, *to give up, to give out, to give over,* &c. This circumftance contributes greatly towards making our lan-guage peculiarly difficult to foreigners.

Notwithftanding the rules of the compofition and derivation of words be ever fo well fixed, cuftom prefcribes how far we may take advantage of them ; and the force of affociation of ideas is hardly any where more evident, than in the difagree-able fenfation excited by words, which, though perfectly intelligible, have not happened to be adopted by the generality of writers ; and efpecially when eafier words have happened to fupply their places.

DERIVATION. 143

places. A few examples will make this remark ftriking. *Damningnefs.* Hammond. *Criminoufnefs.* King Charles. *Defignlefsly.* Boyle, *Candidnefs.* South. *The naturalnefs of the thought.* Addifon on Medals, p. 84. *Defcanting upon the value, rarity, and* authenticalnefs *of the feveral pieces that lie before them.* Ib. *The fcience of medals, which is charged with fo many* unconcerning *parts of knowledge.* Ib. 84. *Among other* informalities. Hume's Hift. vol. 4. p. 401. *It would be fuch a* difobligation *to the prince.* Ib. vol. 6. p. 74. *The* diflikers *may be forced to fall in with.* Swift. *To difcover its fpirit and* intendment. Law Tracts, Pref. p. 9. *Without any* circuity. Hume. ‹ Inftead of *precipitate,* and *precipitately,* Mr. Hume writes *precipitant.* Hiftory, vol. 8. p. 281. and *precipitantly.* Ib. p. 291. Alfo inftead for *confultation,* he ufes *confult.* Ib. vol. 8. p. 65. *It would be unnatural, and* incomfortable. Law Tracts, vol. 6. p. 125. *It would have been too* impopular *among the Spaniards.* Bolingbroke on Hiftory, vol. 2. p. 11.

Latin prefixes and terminations do not well fuit with Saxon words, and *vice verfa.* *Deflikenefs.* Locke. For this reafon, *difqiuetnefs* is not fo good a word as *difquietude,*

tude, or *inquietude*. There are, however, several exceptions to this obfervation; as the word *genuinenefs*.

I wifh we had more liberty to introduce new words, by a derivation analogous to others already in ufe, when they are evidently wanted. We have, for inftance, no term to exprefs a perfon who underftands mechanics. A *mechanic* is a mere workman. And yet I am afraid that *mechanift*, which Mr. Johnfon has introduced in this fenfe, will not be generally adopted. *Having feen what a* mechanift *had already performed*. Raffelas, vol. i. p. 36.

When there are two derivatives from the fame word, they are apt to flide, by degrees into different meanings; a cuftom which tends greatly to enrich a language. Thus we ufe the word *adhefion* in a literal fenfe; as when we fpeak of the adhefion of the lungs to the pleura; and we ufe the word *adherence* in a figurative fenfe only; as when we fpeak of the adherence of a people to their prince, or to a caufe. We alfo ufe the word *expofure* in a literal fenfe, and *expofition* in a figurative one; yet Mr. Hume fays, *a fountain which has a* north expofition. Political Effays, p. 219.

Though

Though both the words *propofal* and *propofition* be derived from the verb *pro-pofe*, we now ufe the word *propofal* to denote a thing that is propofed to be done, and *propofition* for an affertion propofed to be proved. Some writers, however, and particularly Mrs. Macaulay, in conformity, perhaps, to the French idiom, ufe the latter in the fenfe of the former. *This obfervation was followed by a propofition, which had been at firft fuggefted, and was immediately confented to by the commiffioners.* Macaulay's Hiftory, vol. 4. p. 312.

The Latin word *extempore* is often ufed without any change, as an Englifh word. Mr. Hume writes *extemporary*. Hift. vol. 6. p. 335.

Derivation is no certain rule to judge of the fenfe of words. The word *humourift* does not fignify a *man of humour*.

There is an inconvenience in introducing new words by compofition which nearly refemble others in ufe before ; as, *differve*, which is too much like *deferve*.

SECTION VIII.

Of Articles.

ARTICLES are, ſtrictly ſpeaking, adjectives, as they neceſſarily require
a noun ſubſtantive to follow them, the
ſignification of which they ſerve to limit
and aſcertain, as all adjectives do.

In ſome few caſes, after the manner
of the French, we prefix the definite article *the* to the names of towns ; as, the
Hague, the *Havannah*, the *Deviſes*.

Proper names, when they are uſed as
common ones, may have an article. *One
would take him to be* an *Achilles*. Devil
upon Crutches.

The article *a* is made more emphatical
by the addition of the adjective *certain*.
A certain man had two ſons. Luke. But
this does not ſeem to ſuit proper names.
At laſt, a certain *Fitzgerald appeared*.
Hume's Hiſtory, vol. 8. p. 161. *One
Fitzgerald* would have been better.

In uſing proper names, we generally
have recourſe to the adjective *one*, to
particulariſe them. If I tell my friend,
I have ſeen one Mr. Roberts, I ſuppoſe the
Mr.

Mr. Roberts that I mean to be a ſtranger to him; whereas, if I ſay, *I have ſeen Mr. Roberts*, I ſuppoſe him to be a perſon well known. Nothing ſuppoſes greater notoriety than to call a perſon ſimply Mr. It is, therefore, great preſumption, or affectation, in a writer, to prefix his name in this manner to any performance, as if all the world were well acquainted with his name and merit.

In general, it may be ſufficient to pre-fix the article to the former of two words in the ſame conſtruction; tho' the French never fail to repeat it in this caſe. *There were many hours, both of the night and day, which he could ſpend, without ſuſpicion, in ſolitary thought.* Raſſelas, vol. 1. p. 23. It might have been, *of* the *night, and of* the *day.* And, for the ſake of emphaſis, we often repeat the article in a ſeries of epithets. *He hoped, that this title would ſecure him a perpetual, and an independent authority.* Hume's Hiſtory, vol. 3. p. 326.

We ſometimes, after the manner of the French, repeat the ſame article when the adjective, on account of any clauſe de-pending upon it, is put after the ſubſtan-tive. *Of all the conſiderable governments among the Alps, a commonwealth is a con-*

ſtitution,

148 ENGLISH GRAMMAR.

ftitution, the *moft adapted of any to the po-
verty of thofe countries*. Addifon on Medals.
*With fuch a fpecious title, as that of blood,
which with the multitude is always the claim,
the ftrongeft, and moft eafily comprehended.*
Ib. p. 235. *They are not the men in the
nation,* the *moft difficult to be replaced.*
Devil upon Crutches.

We fometimes repeat the article, when
the epithet precedes the fubftantive. *He
was met by* the *worfhipful* the *magiftrates.*

It fhould feem, that as *a* without *n* is
prefixed to a confonant, it ought to fuffice
before an *h* that is founded, which is, generally, equivalent to a confonant; yet
many writers prefix *an* to words beginning
with that letter. *An half.* Blackftone's
Commentaries. *Beings of* an *higher order.*
Raffelas, vol. 1. p. 112.

A is fometimes put for *every*; as in
fuch phrafes as thefe, *a hundred* a *year*,
i. e. *every year*; or for *one*, as when we fay,
fo much a *dozen,* a *pound,* &c. *A hundred men* a *day died of it.* Hume's Hiftory, vol. 5. p. 80. The French always
ufe the article *the* in this conftruction. It
appears, however, that the article *a*, which,
in many cafes, fignifies *one*, fhould not be
prefixed to words which exprefs a great
number, yet cuftom authorifes this ufe of
it.

it. *Liable to* a great many *inconveniencies.*
Tillotſon. *Many a man,* i. e. *many times a
man.*

A nice diſtinction of the ſenſe is ſometimes made by the uſe or omiſſion of the
article *a.* If I ſay, *He behaved with* a
little reverence, my meaning is poſitive.
If I ſay, *He behaved with little reverence,*
my meaning is negative ; and theſe two
are by no means the ſame, or to be uſed
in the ſame caſes. By the former I rather
praiſe a perſon, by the latter I diſpraiſe
him.

For the ſake of this diſtinction, which is
a very uſeful one, we may better bear the
ſeeming impropriety of this article *a* before nouns of number. When I ſay *there
were* few men *with him,* I ſpeak diminu-
tively, and mean to repreſent them as in-
conſiderable. Whereas, when I ſay *There
were* a few men *with him,* I evidently in-
tend to make the moſt of them.

Sometimes a nice diſtinction may be
made in the ſenſe by a regard to the
poſition of the article only. When we ſay
half a crown, we mean a piece of money of
one half of the value of a crown ; but
when we ſay *a half crown* we mean a
half crown piece, or a piece of metal,

of

of a certain fize, figure, &c. Two fhil-
lings and fix pence is *half a crown,* but
not *a half crown.*

The article *the* is often elegantly put,
after the manner of the French, for the
pronoun poffeffive. As, *he looks him full
in* the *face,* i. e. *in his face. That awful
Majefty, in whofe prefence they were to
ftrike* the *forehead on the ground,* i. e.
their foreheads. Fergufon on Civil Society,
p. 390.

Some writers, according to the fame
idiom, drop the article *the* before titles,
and write (for they would not fay) *preface,
introduction, dedication,* &c. inftead of, *the
preface, the introduction, the dedication,* &c.
which is the true Englifh idiom.

In applying the ordinal numbers to
a feries of kings, &c. we generally inter-
pofe the article *the* between the name
and the adjective expreffing the number,
as, *Henry* the *firft, Charles* the *fecond ;* but
fome writers affect to tranfpofe thefe words,
and place the numeral adjective firft.
The firft Henry. Hume's Hiftory, vol. 1.
p. 497. This conftruction is common
with this writer, but there feems to be
a familiarity and want of dignity in it.

The

The article *the* has, fometimes, a fine effect, in diftinguifhing a perfon by an epithet; as it gives us an idea of him, as being the only perfon to whom it can be applied. *In the hiftory of Henry the fourth, by father Daniel, we are furprized at not finding him* the *great man.* Smollett's Voltaire, vol. 5. p. 82. *I own, I am often furprized you fhould have treated fo coldly, a man, fo much* the *gentleman.* Fair American, vol. 1. p. 13. Sometimes this fame article is ufed in converfation, with a peculiar kind of emphafis, fimilar to the cafes above-mentioned; as, *He was never* the *man, that gave me a penny in his whole life.*

When a word is in fuch a ftate, as that it may, with very little impropriety, be confidered, either as a proper, or a common name, the article *the* may be prefixed to it or not, at pleafure. *The Lord Darnly was the perfon in whom moft men's wifhes centered.* Hume's Hiftory, vol. 5. p. 87. *Lord Darnly* would have read juft as well; and this form is more common, the word *Lord* being generally confidered as part of the proper name.

Formerly, the article *the* was prefixed to the pronoun relative. *In* the *which*, Corinthians.

H 4   For

For the greater emphafis, degrees of comparifon frequently take this article. The oftener *I read this author*, the more *I admire him. I think his ftyle* the beft I *ever read*.

In a variety of phrafes, in which the fenfe is abftract, or the fentence contracted, articles are omitted. As, *he went on foot, or on horfeback.* In many of thefe cafes, it is not improbable, but that the articles were ufed originally ; but were dropped when the phrafes became familiar. Thus *by fea*, *by land*, *on fhore*, &c. might have been, *by the fea, by the land, on the fhore*, &c. When fuch phrafes as thefe are very familiar, we do not expect an article, and are rather difappointed when we find one. *The half-learned man, relying upon his ftrength, feldom perceives his wants, till he finds his deception* paft a cure. Hiftory of England in Letters, vol. 1. p. 41. We generally fay, *paft cure.* When words are ufed, in this manner, without any article, it is a pretty fure fign, that they are, or have been, in frequent ufe. *The rights and immunities* of holy church. Parliamentary Hiftory, vol. 1. p. 12.

When the names of things are fo circumftanced, that articles, and other marks of particularity, are unneceffary ; we ufually

ally omit them, efpecially in converfation.
A familiar example of this we may obferve in perfons fpeaking to children, who
generally fay, *nurfe, pappa,* or *mamma*;
and feldom *your nurfe, your pappa,* or *your
mamma*; becaufe the child has no idea of
any nurfe, &c. befides his own.

In many other cafes, the articles feem
to be omitted where we can difcover nothing but a mere ellipfis; as no reafon
can be feen for the omiffion, except that
it has a little more concifenefs or energy.
Thus we fay, *Have you trout in this river,*
i. e. *have you any of that fpecies of fifh which
is called trout. Nothing is fo dangerous, as
to unite two perfons fo clofely, in all their
interefts and concerns, as* man and wife,
without rendering the union entire and total.
Hume's Effays, p. 259. *He was fired
with the defire of doing fomething, tho' he
knew not yet, with diftinctnefs, either* end
or means. Raffelas, vol. 1. p. 22. In
the former of thefe fentences, the words
a man and his wife would have conveyed
the fame idea, and in the fame extent, as
man and wife; for the meaning of both is
precifely, *any man and his wife.* In the
latter fentence, *the end and the means* would
have expreffed the idea very completely,

fince

fince only one particular end or means was intended.

In the following fentence an univerfality feems to be aimed at by the omiffion of the article, which the fenfe hardly requires. *The pope found himfelf entitled to the pof-feffion of England and Ireland, on account of the herefy of prince and people.* Of the *prince* would have been better. In fome cafes, however, there feems to be a peculiar elegance in adopting the univerfal fenfe of the word, by omitting the article when it might have been ufed with propriety enough. *If the young man who appeared in Flanders was really fon to king Edward, he never would bear arms againft him.* Hume's Hiftory, vol. 3. p. 383. Perhaps the following fentence is rather more elegant by the omiffion of the article. *I fufpect, that from any height where life can be fupported, there may be danger of too quick defcent.* Raffelas, vol. 1. p. 39. *Too quick a defcent* is more common.

In many cafes, articles are omitted in common converfation, or in familiar ftyle, which feem to have a propriety in writing, or in grave ftyle. At worft, *time might be gained by this expedient.* Hume's Hiftory, vol. 6. p. 435. *At the worft* might have

have been better in this place. In very familiar ſtyle we ſometimes drop the article after it has been frequently uſed. *Give me here John Baptiſt's head.* There would have been more dignity in ſaying, *John the Baptiſt's head.*

SECTION IX.

Of the Uſe of Prepoſitions.

ALL that I have done in this difficult part of grammar, concerning the proper uſe of prepoſitions, has been to make a few general remarks upon the ſubjeᏟ; and then to give a collection of the inſtances, that have occurred to me, of the improper uſe of ſome of them. To make a grammar complete, every verb, and adjective, to which theſe prepoſitions are ever ſubjoined, ought to be reduced into tables; in which all the variety of caſes in which they are uſed, ſhould be carefully diſtinguiſhed. The greateſt part of ſuch tables, however, would be of little uſe to Engliſh men, who are generally accuſtomed to the right prepoſition;

and who will be chiefly liable to make miftakes where others have been miftaken before them ; and a confiderable number of thefe cafes I have noted.

Different relations, and different fenfes, muft be expreffed by different prepofitions ; tho' in conjunction with the fame verb or adjective. Thus we fay, *to converfe* with *a perfon*, upon *a fubject*, in *a houfe*, &c. We alfo fay, *we are difappointed* of *a thing*, when we cannot get it ; and *difappointed* in *it*, when we have it, and find it does not anfwer our expectations. But two different prepofitions muft be improper in the fame conftruction, and in the fame fentence. *The combat* between *thirty Britons*, againft *twenty Englifh*. Smollett's Voltaire, vol. 2. p. 292.

In fome cafes, it is not poffible to fay to which of two prepofitions the preference is to be given, as both are ufed promifcuoufly, and cuftom has not decided in favour of either of them. We fay, *expert* at, and *expert* in *a thing*. *Expert at finding a remedy for his miftakes*. Hume's Hift. vol. 4. p. 417. We fay, *difapproved* of, and *difapproved* by *a perfon*. *Difapproved* by *our court*. Swift. It is not improbable, but that, in time, thefe different conftructions may be appropriated to different

ferent uſes. All languages furniſh examples of this kind, and the Engliſh as many
as any other.

When prepoſitions are ſubjoined to
nouns, they are generally the ſame which
are ſubjoined to the verbs, from which
the nouns are derived. *John, ſhewing the
ſame diſpoſition to tyranny* over *his ſubjeEts.*
Hume's Hiſt. vol. 1. p. 74. i. e. *to ty-
rannize* over *his ſubjeEts.*

When a word ending in *ing* is preceded
by an article, it ſeems to be uſed as a
noun; and therefore ought not to govern another word, without the intervention of a prepoſition. *By blackening
his fame, had that injury been in their power,
they formed a very proper prelude to* the murdering *his perſon.* Hume's Hiſtory, vol. 7.
p. 117. In this conſtruEtion, the word
murdering is evidently a párticiple of an
aEtive verb. Qu. alſo, is *murdering a
man's perſon* proper?

The force of a prepoſition is implied
in ſome words, particularly in the word
kome. When we ſay, *he went kome,* we
mean to *his own houſe;* yet in other con-
ſtruEtions, this ſame word requires a prepoſition; for we ſay, *he went* from home.

Many writers affeEt to ſubjoin to any
word the prepoſition with which it is compounded,

pounded, or the idea of which it implies;
in order to point out the relation of the
words in a more diftinct and definite
manner; and to avoid the more indeter-
minate prepofitions *of*, and *to* ; but general practice, and the idiom of the Englifh
tongue, feem to oppofe the innovation.
Thus many writers fay *averfe* from *a thing*.
Averfe from *Venus*. Pope. *The abhorrence* againft *all other fects*. Hume's Hiftory, vol. 4. p. 34. But other writers
ufe *averfe* to *it*, which feems more
truly Englifh. *Averfe* to *any advice*.
Swift. An attention to the latent metaphor may be pleaded in favour of the
former example, and this is a rule of general ufe, in directing what prepofitions
to fubjoin to a word. Thus we fay *devolve*
upon *a thing*, and Mr. Addifon improperly
fays, *poetical imitation*, founded in [on]
*natural refemblance, is much inferior to that
of painting*. But this rule would fometimes miflead us, particularly where the
figure has become nearly evanefcent.
Thus we fhould naturally expect, that
the word *depend* would require *from* after
it ; but cuftom obliges us to fay *depend
upon*, as well as *infift upon a thing*. Yet
were we to ufe the fame word where the
figure was manifeft, we fhould ufe the
prepo-

prepofition *from*; as *the cage* depends from *the roof of the building*.

Of the Prepofition of.

Several of our modern writers have leaned to the French idiom in the ufe of the prepofition *of*, by applying it where the French ufe *de*, tho' the Englifh idiom would require another prepofition, or no prepofition at all in the cafe ; but no writer has departed more from the genius of the Englifh tongue, in this refpect, than Mr. Hume. *Richlieu profited of every circumftance, which the conjuncture afforded.* Hume's Hiftory, vol. 4. p. 251. We fay *profited* by. *He remembered him of the fable.* Ib. vol. 5. p. 185. The *great difficulty they find* of *fixing juft fentiments*. Ib. *The king of England, provided* of *every fupply*. Ib. vol. 1. p. 206. In another place he writes, *provide them* in *food and raiment*. Ib. vol. 2. p. 65. The true Englifh idiom feems to be *to provide* with *a thing*. *It is fituation chiefly which* decides of *the fortunes and characters of men* Ib. vol. 6. p. 283. i. e. *concerning*. *He found the greateft difficulty* of *writing*. Ib. vol. 1. p. 401. i. e. in. Of *which, he was extremely greedy, extremely prodigal, and extremely*

160 ENGLISH GRAMMAR.

tremely neceffitous. Ib. vol. 4. p. 13.
He was eager *of recommending it to his
fellow-citizens.* Ib. vol. 7. p. 161. *The
good Lady was careful of* ferving me of
every thing. In this example *with* would
have been more proper.

It is agreeable to the fame idiom, that
of feems to be ufed inftead of *for* in the
following fentences. *The rain hath been
falling of a long time.* Maupertuis' Voyage, p. 60. *It might perhaps have given
me a greater tafte of its antiquities.* Addifon. *Of,* in this place, occafions a real
ambiguity in the fenfe. *A tafte* of a *thing*
implies actual enjoyment of it ; but *a tafte*
for *it* only implies a capacity for enjoyment. *The efteem which Philip had conceived of the ambaffador.* Hume's Hiftory,
vol. 6. p. 40. *You know the efteem I have*
of *this philofophy.* Law Tracts, vol. 1.
p. 3. *Youth wandering in foreign countries,
with as little refpect of others, as prudence
of his own, to guard him from danger. An
indemnity of paft offences.* Hume's Hiftory,
vol. 5. p. 20.

In the following fentences, *on* or *upon*
might very well be fubftituted for *of.
Was totally dependent of the papal crown.*
Hume's Hiftory, vol. 2. p. 71. *Laid
hold* of. Ib. vol. 1. p. 292. We alfo
ufe

uſe *of* inſtead of *on* or *upon*, in the following familiar phraſes, which occur chiefly
in converſation; *to call* of *a perſon*, and *to
wait* of *him.*

In ſome caſes, a regard to the French
idiom hath taught us to ſubſtitute *of* for
in. The great difficulty they found of *fixing
juſt ſentiments.* Hume's Hiſtory, vol. 6.
p. 63. *Curious* of *Antiquities.* Dryden.

In a variety of caſes, the prepoſition *of*
ſeems to be ſuperfluous in our language;
and, in moſt of them, it has been derived
to us from the French. *Notwithſtanding*
of *the numerous panegyrics on the antient
Engliſh liberty.* Hume's Eſſays, p. 81.
Notwithſtanding of *this unlucky example.*
Ib p. 78. Aukward as this conſtruction
is, it is generally uſed by ſeveral of our
later writers. This prepoſition ſeems to
be ſuperfluous, when it is prefixed to a
word which is only uſed to ſhow the extent of another preceding word, as, *the
city of London, the paſſions of hope and fear
are very ſtrong.* It alſo ſeems to be ſuperfluous after ſeveral adjectives, which are
ſometimes uſed as ſubſtantives, *a dozen of*
years. Hume's Eſſays, p. 258.

In the following inſtances, it may be a
matter of indifference whether we uſe this
prepoſition or not. *To one who conſiders*
cooly

coolly of *the fubject.* Hume's Political Effays, p. 141. *I can conceive of nothing
more worthy of him.* Price. It is fometimes omitted, and fometimes inferted after
worthy. It is worthy obfervation. Hume's
Hiftory. I fhould chufe to make ufe of
it in this cafe. But I think it had better
be omitted in the following fentence.
*The emulation who fhould ferve their country
beft no longer fubfifts among them, but of who
fhould obtain the moft lucrative command.*
Montague's Rife and Fall of antient Republicks, p. 137. The whole conftruction
of this fentence is by no means natural.
The meaning of it, when expreffed at full
length is, *The emulation which confifts in
ftriving who fhould ferve his country,* &c.

The prepofition *of* feems to be omitted
in the following fentence, in which it re-
fembles the French idiom. *All this, however, is eafily learned from medals, where they
may fee likewife the plan of many, the moft
confiderable buildings of antient Rome.* Addifon on Medals, p. 23. i. e. *of many* of
the moft confiderable buildings, &c.

Of is frequently ambiguous, and would
oftener be perceived to be fo, did not the
fenfe of the reft of the paffage in which it
occurs prevent that inconvenience; and
this it will often do, even when this part
of

of the fentence, fingly taken, would fuggeſt a meaning the very reverfe of what is intended. *The attack* of *the Engliſh* naturally means *an attack made by the Engliſh, upon others*; but in the following fentence, it means an attack made upon the Engliſh. *The two princes concerted the means of rendering ineffectual their common attack* of *the Engliſh.* Hume's Hiſtory, vol. 3. p. 114. *The oppreſſion* of *the peaſants feemeth great*, p. 152. is in itſelf quite ambiguous, but the fenſe of the paſſage make the peaſants to be the oppreſſed, not the oppreſſors.

Of is uſed in a particular fenſe in the phraſe, *he is* of *age*, the meaning of which is, *he is arrived at what is deemed the age of manhood.*

Of the Prepoſitions to *and* for.

Agreeably to the Latin and French idioms, the prepoſition *to* is fometimes uſed in conjunction with ſuch words as, in thoſe languages, govern the dative caſe ; but this conſtruction does not ſeem to ſuit the Engliſh language. *His ſervants ye are,* to *whom ye obey.* Romans. *And* to *their general's voice they ſoon obeyed.* Milton. *The people of England may congratulate* to *them-*

*themselves, that the nature of our govern-
ment, and the clemency of our kings secure
us.* Dryden. *Something like this has been
reproached* to *Tacitus.* Bolingbroke on
History, vol. 1. p. 136.

To seems to be used instead of *for* in the
following sentences. *Deciding law-suits* to
the northern counties. Hume's History,
vol. 4 p. 191. *A great change* to *the
better.* Hume's Essays, p. 133. At least
for is more usual in this construction.

To seems to be used improperly in the
following sentences. *His abhorrence* to
that superstitious figure. Hume's History,
vol. 6. p. 223. i. e. *of. Thy prejudice* to
my cause. Dryden. i. e. *against. Conse-
quent* to. Locke. i. e. *upon. The English
were very different people then* to *what they
are at present.* Smollett's Voltaire, vol. 1.
p. 178.

In compliance to *the declaration of the
English parliament.* Macaulay's History,
vol. 4. p. 57.

In several cases, *to* may be suppressed ;
but if there be two clauses of a sentence,
in the same construction, it should either
be omitted, or inserted in both alike. *The
people stole his gibbet, and paid it the same
veneration, as* to *his cross.* Hume's Hist.
vol. 2. p. 39

The

The place of the prepofition *for*, might
have been better fupplied by other prepofitions in the following fentences. *The
worfhip of this deity is extremely ridiculous,
and therefore better* adapted for *the vulgar.*
Smollett's Voltaire, vol. 1. p. 203. i. e. *to.
To die* for *thirft.* Addifon. i. e. *of* or *by.
More than they* thought for [of]. D'Alem-
bert's Hiftory of the Expulfion of the Je-
fuit's, p. 132. *I think that virtue is fo a-
miable in herfelf, that there is no need* for [of]
*the knowledge of God, to make her beloved
and followed.* Smollett's Voltaire, vol. 1.
p. 30. *If the party chufe to* infift for [upon]
it. Law Tracts, vol. 1. p. 70.

The prepofition *for*, is ufed in a peculiar fenfe in the following paffage ; *and
prejudices for prejudices fome perfons may
be apt to think, that thofe of a churchman
are as tolerable as of any other.* Law Tracts,
vol. 1. p. 184. i. e. *if prejudices on all fides
be fairly compared.*

For is fuperfluous in the phrafe, *more
than he knows for.* Shakefpear. This is
only ufed in familiar and colloquial ftyle.

Of the Prepofitions with *and* upon.

The prepofition *with* feems to be ufed
where *to* would have been more proper in
the

the following fentences. *Reconciling him-self* with *the king.* Hume's Hiftory, vol 4. p. 176. *Thofe things which have the greateſt* refemblance with *each other frequently differ the moſt.* Smollett's Voltaire, vol. 3. p. 65. *And that fuch feleĉtion, and rejeĉtion ſhould be* confonant with *our proper nature.* Harris's three Treatifes, p. 205. *Conformable with.* Addifon. *The hiſtory of St. Peter is* agreeable with *the facred text.* Newberry's New Teſtament.

Other prepofitions had better have been fubftituted for *with* in the following fentences. *Glad* with [*at*] *the fight of hoſtile blood.* Dryden. *He has as much reafon to be angry* with *you as* with *him.* Preceptor, vol. 1. p. 10. *Converfant* with *a fcience:* Pope. *In* would have been at leaſt equally proper. *They could be prevailed* with [*upon*] *to retire.* Hume's Hiſtory, vol. 4. p. 10.

In the following fentence *to difpenſe* with *myfelf* is ufed in the fame fenfe as *to excufe myfelf. I could not difpenfe with myfelf from making a voyage to Caprea.* Addifon.

The prepofition *with* and a perfonal pronoun fometimes ferve for a contraĉtion of a claufe of a fentence. *The homunculus is endowed with the fame locomotive powers and faculties* with *us.* Triſtram Shandy, vol.

vol, 1. p. 5. i, e. *the same faculties with which we are endowed.*

The oblique case of the personal pronouns is used in conjunction with this preposition by way of emphasis, without any other addition to the sense, as *away* with *thee, get thee gone* with *thee.*

The preposition *on* or *upon* seems to be used improperly in the following sentences. *I thank you for helping me to an use* (of a medal) *that perhaps I should not have* thought on [of]. Addison on Medals. *Authors have to* brag on [of]. Pope. *Censorious* upon *all his brethren.* Swift. perhaps *of. His reason could not attain a thorough conviction* on *those subjects.* Hume's History, vol. 7. p. 355. *A greater quantity may be taken from the heap, without making any sensible alteration* upon it. Hume's Political Essays, p. 12. i. e. *in. Every office of command should be entrusted to persons* on [in] *whom the parliament could confide.* Macaulay's History, vol. 3. p. 112.

This preposition seems to be superfluous in the following sentence. *Their efforts seemed to anticipate* on *the spirit, which became so general afterwards.* Hume's Hist. vol. 3. p. 5.

We say, *to* depend upon *a thing,* but not *to* promise upon *it. But this effect we may safely fafely fay, no one could beforehand have* promifed upon. Hume's Hiftory, vol. 8. p. 75. It might have been, *have promifed themfelves.*

Of the Prepofitions in, from, and others.

The prepofition *in* is fometimes ufed where the French ufe their *en*, but where fome other prepofition would be more agreeable to the Englifh idiom. Some of the following fentences are examples of this. *He made a point of honour in* [*of*] *not departing from his enterprize.* Hume's Hiftory, vol. 1. p. 402. *I think it necef-fary, for the intereft of virtue and religion, that the whole kingdom fhould le informed* in *fome parts of your character.* Swift. i. e. *about,* or *concerning.* In fome of thefe cafes, *in* might with advantage be changed for *to* or *into*. *Painters have not a little contributed to bring the ftudy of medals* in *vogue.* Addifon. On the other hand, I have found *into* put for *in* : *engaged him* into *attempts.* Hume's Hiftory, vol. 5 p. 162. *To be liable in a compenfation.* Law Tracts, vol. 1. p. 45.

It is agreeable to the French idiom, that *in* is fometimes put for *with*. *H had*

been

been provided in *a small living by the Duke of Norfolk.* Hume's History, vol. 8. p. 68.

In some familiar cafes, there is an ellipfis of this prepofition. *It was esteemed no wife probable.* Hume's History, vol. 7. p. 315. but this conftruction hardly fuits grave ftyle.

In is fuperfluous in the colloquial phrafe, *he finds me* in *money and cloaths*, &c.

The prepofition *from* had better be changed in the following fentences. *The eftates of all were burthened by fines and confifcations, which had been levied* from *them.* Hume's History, vol. 7. p. 315. *He acquits me* from *mine iniquity.* Job. better *of. Could he have profited* from [by] *repeated experiences.* Hume's History, vol. 8. p. 239.

From feems to be fuperfluous after *forbear. He could not forbear* from *appointing the Pope to be one if the God fathers.* Ib. vol. 8. p. 282.

The prepofition *among* always implies a number of things; and, therefore, cannot be ufed in conjunction with the word *every*, which is in the fingular number. *Which is found* among every *fpecies of liberty.* Hume's Effays, p. 92. *The opinion of the advance of riches in the ifland*

I   *feems*

feems to gain ground among every body.
Hume's Political Effays, p. 71.

There feems to be fome impropriety in the ufe of the prepofition *under* in the following fentence. *That range of hills, known* under *the general name of mount Jura.* Account of Geneva.

The prepofition *through* is fometimes fupplied by a very particular conftruction of the adjective *long,* thus *all night long,* and *all day long,* are equivalent to, *through all the night, through all the day.*

Sometimes *a* is put for *in. But the Baffa detains us till he receives orders from Adrianople, which may probably be* a month a coming. Lady Montague's Letters, vol. 1. p. 147. i. e. *in coming.*

SECTION X.

Of the Order of Words in a Sentence.

AN adjective fhould not be feparated from its fubftantive, even by words which modify its meaning, and make but one fenfe with it. *A* large enough num-

8   ber

ber *furely.* Hume's Political Effays, p.
196. *a number large enough* *The lower
fort of people are* good enough judges
of one not very diftant from them. Ib. p.
261. *Ten thoufand is* a large enough bafe.
Ib.

Adjectives fignifying dimenfions, and
fome other properties of things, come after the nouns expreffing thofe particular
dimenfions, or properties. *A tree three
feet thick. A body fifty thoufand ftrong.*
Hume's Hiftory, vol. 3. p. 242. This
laft expreffion is rather vulgar.

There is, fometimes, great elegance,
as well as force, in placing the adjective
before the verb, and the fubftantive immediately after it ; as, Great *is the* Lord,
juft *and* true *are thy* ways, *thou king of
faints.* It gives a poetical elevation to the
expreffion.

Sometimes the word *all* is emphatically
put after a number of particulars comprehended under it.

*Her fury, her defpair, her every gefture
Was nature's language* all.

               Voltaire, vol. 27. p. 274.
Ambition, intereft, glory, all *concurred.*
Letters on Chivalry, p. 11. Sometimes
a fubftantive, which, likewife, comprehends the preceding particulars, is ufed

                      in

in conjunction with this adjective. *Royalists, republicans, churchmen, 'sectaries, courtiers, patriots* ; all parties *concurred in the illusion.* Hume's History, vol. 8. p. 73.

The word *such* is often placed after a number of particulars to which it equally relates. *The figures of discourse, the pointed antithesis, the unnatural conceit, the jingle of words* ; such *false ornaments were not employed by early writers.* Hume's History, vol. 6. p. 129.

By way of emphasis, the demonstrative pronoun *this,* though in the construction of a nominative case, is sometimes placed without any verb, after the words to which it belongs. *A matter of great importance* this, *in the conduct of life.* I cannot say that I admire this construction, though it be much used, and particularly, if I remember right, by Mr. Seed, in his sermons.

Words designed to distinguish, and to give an emphasis to the personal pronouns, which are the nominative case to a verb, are naturally placed after it. *If ye forgive not, every one of you, h s brother his trespasses.*

When a sentence begins with the words *all, many, so, as, how, too,* and perhaps
some

some others, the article *a* is elegantly preceded by the adjective, and followed by its correspondent substantive. *He spake in so affecti nate a m inner.* So *tall a man I never saw before.* So *profeſſed* an *aamirer of the ancient poets.* Addiſon on Medals, p. 27. *He is too great a man.*

Moſt other particles muſt be placed before the adjectives ; as, *he ſpake in* quite an *affectionate manner. Such a dark cloud overcaſt the evening of that day.* Hume's Hiſtory, vol. 5. p. 469. So *dark a cloud* would have been equivalent, and in all reſpects better. *He was no leſs able a negociator, than a courageous warrier.* Smollett's Voltaire, vol. 1. p. 181.

The prepoſition *of* will not bear to be ſeparated from the noun which it either precedes or follows, without a diſagreeable effect. *The ignorance of that age, in mechanical arts, rendered* the progreſs *very ſlow* of *this new invention.* Hume's Hiſtory, vol. 2. p 445. *Being in no ſenſe capable* of *either* intention *or remiſſion.* Harris's three Treatiſes, p. 190. *The* word *itſelf* of·*God. His* picture, *in diſtemper,* of *calumny borrow'd from the deſcription of one painted by Apelles, was ſuppoſed to be a ſatyr on that cardinal.* Walpole's Aneedotes.

The country first dawned, that illuminated the world, and beyond which the arts *cannot be traced,* of *civil society or domestic life.* Raffelas, vol. 2. p. 32.

Little explanatory circumstances are particularly aukward between a genitive case, and the word which usually follows it. *She began to extol the* farmer's, *as she called him,* excellent underftanding. Harriot Watfon, vol. 1. p. 27.

If an entire claufe of a fentence depend upon a word followed by *of,* the tranfpofition is eafy. *Few* examples *occur,* of *princes who have willingly refigned their power.* Hume's Hiftory, vol. 5. p. 472. If the words followed by this particle make a claufe, which might have been omitted, and have left the fenfe compleat, it may be inferted at fome diftance from the noun on which they depend, as it were, by way of parenthefis. *The noblest* difcoveries *thofe authors ever made,* of *art or of nature, have all been produced by the tranfcendent genius of the prefent age.* Swift's Tale of a Tub, p. 57.

The prepofition *of,* and the words with which it is connected, may often elegantly precede the verb on which they both depend. *Two months had now paffed, and of Pekuah nothing had been heard.*
Raf-

Raffelas, vol. 2. p. 54. Thisconftruction
is not quite fo eafy, when thefe words depend upon a fubftantive coming after
them. *He found the place replete with won-*
ders, of which *he propofed to folace himfelf*
with the contemplation, *if he fhould never*
be able to accomplifh his flight. Ib. vol. 1.
p. 32. This conftruction is properly
French, and does not fucceed very well in
Englifh. Of the prefent ftate, *whatever*
it be, we feel and are forced to confefs the
mifery. Ib. p. 143. In the former of
thefe fentences we fhould read, *with the*
contemplation of which he propofed to folace
himfelf. I am glad, then, fays Cynthio, that
he has thrown him upon a fcience, of which
ke has long wifhed to hear the ufefulnefs.
Addifon on Medals, p. 12.

It is a matter of indifference, with refpect to the pronoun *one another*, whether
the prepofition *of* be placed between the
two parts of it, or before them both. We
may either fay, *they were jealous* one of another, or *they were jealous* of one another.

Whenever no ambiguity will be occafioned by putting the nominative cafe after
the verb, this conftruction makes an elegant variety in Englifh ftyle. This is particularly the cafe in verbs neuter, which
admit of no object of the affirmation.

Upon

Upon thy right hand ſtands *the* Queen. The nominative caſe has always this place when a ſentence begins with the particle *there*. There was a man *ſent from God, whoſe name was John.* And generally after *then*. Then came *unto him the* Phariſees. It may often, in other-caſes, have this place, and even be ſeparated from the verb by other words. *His character is as much diſputed as* is *commonly* that *of princes who are our cotemporaries.* Hume's Hiſtory, vol. 6. p. 97. But they are aukwardly ſeparated in the following ſentence. *Even* the ſavage, *ſtill leſs than the citizen,* can *be made to quit that manner of life, in which he has been trained.* Ferguſon on Civil Society, p. 145.

In the cloſe of a paragraph, the nominative caſe generally follows the verb, even when the ſentence is affirmative. *And thus* have you *exhibited a ſort of a ſketch of art.* Harris's three Treatiſes, p. 12.

But when the nominative caſe is complex, and conſiſts of ſeveral words, it is better to place it before the verb. The following ſentence, in which a different order is obſerved, is ungraceful. *An undertaking, which, in the execution, proved as impracticable,* as had *turned out* every other of their pernicious, yet abortive ſchemes.

fchemes. Macaulay's Hiftory, vol. 4. p. 256

The nominative cafe does not eafily follow the verb when the particle *than* precedes it. *He thought that the prefbyters would foon have become more dangerous to the magiftrate, than* had *ever been* the prelatical clergy. Hume's Hiftory, vol. 7. p. 71. *than the prelatical clergy had ever been.*

When the nominative cafe is put after a verb, the adverb *never*, and fuch others as are ufually placed after the verb, are put before them both ; and when thofe words begin a fentence, we are difappointed, if the verb do not immediately follow it. Never *fovereign* was *bleffed with more moderation of temper.* Hume's Hift. vol. 6. p. 389. *never was fovereign.* Hence the impoffibility appears, *that this undertaking fhould be begun and carried on in a monarchy.* Hume's Effays, p. 173. *hence appears the impoffibility.*

Alfo when the nominative cafe is put after the verb, on account of an interrogation, no other word fhould be interpofed between them. May not we *here fay with Lucretius.* Addifon on Medals, p. 29. may we not *fay.* Is not *it he.* Smollett's Voltaire, vol. 18. p. 152. *is it not he.*

I 5 When

When a nominative cafe is not put after a verb, it has a ftill worfe effect to place the negative particles before it. *Not only he found himfelf a prifoner very narrowly guarded.* Hume's Hiftory, vol. 7. p. 77. It fhould either have been, he *not only found himfelf,* or *not only did he find himfelf.* The following fentence is ftill more aukwardly conftructed, by the interpofition of a claufe between the nominative cafe and the verb. *Not only the power of the crown, by means of wardfhips and purveyance, was very confiderable, it was alfo unequal, and perfonal.* Hume's Hiftory, vol. 7. p. 362.

The auxiliary verb *do,* or *did,* is necef-farily placed before the nominative cafe, when the fentence begins with *neither, nor,* and perhaps fome other adverbs. This rule is obferved in one part of the follow-ing fentence, and neglected in the other. The difference of the effect will be per-ceived by every Englifh ear. *Neither the conftable opened his gates to them, nor did the Duke of Burgundy bring him the fmalleft affiftance.* Hume's Hiftory, vol. 3. p. 266.

By a very peculiar idom, the nomina-tive cafe is fometimes put after the verbs *may, can, &c.* when furprize is expreffed,

or

or a queſtion is reported, &c. the words
if, *whether*, &c. being underſtood, as, *I
wonder*, can he do *it*; i. e. *I wonder whether he can do it. She demanded of me*, could
I play *at cribbage.* Swift's Poſthumous
Works. i. e. *ſhe demanded of me, if I could
play.* I have frequently heard this form
of expreſſion in converſation, but do not
remember ever to have met with it in
writing, except in this paſſage of Swift.

The negative particles are not well ſitu-
ated between the active participles of auxiliary verbs, and the paſſive participles of
other verbs. *Which* being not *admitted
into general uſe*, does not pleaſe the ear ſo
well as *which* not being *admitted.* Having
not *known, or not conſidered*; i. e. not having *known.*

When ſeveral auxiliary verbs are uſed,
the place of the adverb is after the firſt of
them (if the ſecond of them be not a
participle) whether the nominative caſe
come before or after the verb. *The three
graces are always hand in hand, to ſhow us
that theſe three ſhould* be never *ſeparated.*
Addiſon on Medals, p. 29. *ſhould* never
be *ſeparated. And ſince the favour can be
conferred but upon few, the greater number*
will be always *diſcontented.* Raſſelas, vol.
2. p. 9. *will always be.* Shall I be never
ſuf-

fuffered to forget thefe lectures. Ib. vol. 1.
p. 16. *fhall I never be.*

Though the negative participles follow the auxiliary verbs in an interrogation, no other adverbs fhould be placed
there along with them. *Would not then
this art have been wholly unknown.* Harris's three Treatifes, p. 24. *Would not
this art then have been.*

So clofely do we expect every relative
to follow its antecedent, that if the antecedent be a genitive cafe, the other fubftantive cannot be interpofed between
them, without a difagreeable effect. *They
attacked* Northumberland's *houfe,* whom
they put to death. Hume's Hiftory, vol.
3. p. 362: . *He had fufficient exp.rience of
the extreme ardour and impatience of* Henry's *temper,* who *could bear no contradiction.*
Ib. vol. 4. p. 99. *I fhall not confine myfelf to any* man's *rules* that *ever lived.* Triftram Shandy, vol. 1. p. 10.

In the following fentences the relative,
being ftill farther removed from its antecedent, has a ftill worfe effect. *To involve
his minifter, in ruin,* who *had been the
author of it.* Hume's Hift. vol. 4. p. 225.
Primauzeth's *fhip was fet on fire,* who, *finding his deftruction inevitable, bore down upon
the Englifh admiral.* Ib. vol. 3. p. 362.

The

The object of an affirmation fhould not eafily be feparated from its verb by the intervention of other claufes of the fentence. The bad effect of this arrangement may be perceived in the following examples. *Frederick, feeing it was impoffible to* truft, *with fafety,* his life *in the hands of Chriftians, was obliged to take the Mahometans for his guard.* Smollett's Voltaire, vol. 2. p. 73. *The emperor refufed* to convert, *at once,* the truce *into a definitive treaty.* Bolingbroke on Hiftory, vol. 2. p. 310. *Becket could not better* difcover, *than by attacking fo powerful an intereft,* his refolution *to maintain with vigour the rights, real or pretended, of his church.* Hume's Hiftory, vol. 1. p. 415.

Even when a verb and a prepofition, or fome other word, make, as it were, but one compound word, and have but one joint meaning, yet they fhould be feparated in this cafe. *As ran propofed to* invite *back* the king *upon conditions.* Hume's Hiftory, vol. 8. p. 299. *to invite the king back.*

The French always place their adverbs immediately after their verbs, but this order by no means fuits the idiom of the Englifh tongue, yet Mr. Hume has ufed it in his hiftory, almoft without variation.

His

*His government gave courage to the English
barons to* carry farther *their opposition.*
Hume's Hift. vol. 2. p. 46. *Edward ob-
tained a dispensation from his oath, which
the barons had compelled Gaveston to take,
that he would* abjure for ever *the realm.*
Ib. vol. 2. p. 342. *to carry their opposition
farther,* and, *to abjure the realm for ever.*

Sometimes a claufe of a fentence, con-
taining a feparate circumftance, is put in
the place of the adverb. *However, the
miferable remains* were, *in the night,* taken
down. Univerfal Hift. vol. 24. p. 272.

When there are more auxiliaries .than
one, the adverb fhould be placed after
them, immediately before the participle.
Dissertations on the prophecies which have
remarkably been *fulfilled in the world.*
Title page to Dr. Newton's treatife on
the prophecies. This combination appears very irregular and harfh. It fhould
have been, *which have been remarkably
fulfilled.* There are, however, fome adverbs,
in very common ufe, as *always, generally,
often, &c,* which, if we judge by the ear,
are better placed betwixt the auxiliaries ; as, *He* has always been *reckoned an
honeft man. The book* may always be *had
at fuch a place.*

So convenient is the place between the auxiliary verb and the participle for other words, that several adjectives, agreeing with the nominative case, are best inserted there. *They all are invested with the power of punishing.* Account of Geneva, p. 91. *they* are all *invested*.

Too many circumstances are thrown before the nominative case and the verb, in the following sentence. *This is what we mean by the original contract of society, which, though, perhaps,* in no instance it has *ever been formally expressed, at the first institution of a state, yet, in nature, and reason, should always be understood and implied in every act of associating together.* Blackstone's Commentaries, vol. 1. p. 48. The arrangement of this sentence will be rectified by placing the circumstance, *in no instance,* between the auxiliary and the participle; *which though perhaps,* it *has, in no instance, been formally expressed.*

The parts of the word *however,* are often separated by the interposition of an adjective, and the particle *so* is prefixed to the part *ever*; which seems to be much better than to subjoin the adjective to the entire word. *The king,* however little *scrupulous in some respects, was incapable of any thing harsh or barbarous.* Hume's Hist.

184 ENGLISH GRAMMAR.

Hift. vol. 7. p. 468. *how little fcrupulous foever.* *The opinions of that fect ftill kept poffeffion of his mind,* however little *they appeared in his conduct.* Ib. 471. *how little foever.* However much *he might defpife the maxims of the king's adminiftration, he kept a total filence on that fubject.* Ib. vol. 8. p. 267. *how much foever.*

The pronouns *whichfoever, howfoever,* and the like, are alfo elegantly divided by the interpofition of the correfponding fubftantive, and make a better conftruction than *which ever,* &c. without *fo* preceding the fubftantive. *On* which ever fide *the king caft his eyes.* Hume's Hift. vol. 6. p. 350. To my ear, *on which fide foever* founds better.

The active participle, placed before its fubftantive, in imitation of the ablative cafe in Latin, makes a very aukward conftruction in Englifh. *Removing the term from Weftminfter,* fitting the parliament, *was illegal.* Macaulay's Hift. vol. 3. p. 283. *while the parliament was fitting,* or *the parliament being fitting.*

In familiar ftyle, the word *though* clofes a fentence, as it were, elliptically. *Indeed but he did though.* Female Quixote, vol. 1. p. 132.

SECTION

Section XI.

Of the Correspondence of Words expressing Numbers.

A Number of perfons, though confidered in fucceffion, in which cafe
there exifts only one at a time, fhould,
neverthelefs, be fpoken of as in the plural number. *The diffentions it had at home,
with its bifhops, and the violences it fuffered
from without, particularly from its conftant
and inveterate* enemy, the Dukes *of Savoy,
kept it engaged in a perpetual fcene of war
and confufion.* Account of Geneva, p. 19.
enemies.

It is a rule, that two diftinct fubjects of
an affirmation require the verb to be in
the plural number, in the fame manner
as if the affirmation had been made concerning two or more things of the fame
kind. But, notwithftanding this, if the
fubjects of the affirmation be nearly related, the verb is rather better in the fingular number. *Nothing but the* marvellous
and fupernatural hath *any charms for them.*
Idlenefs and ignorance [confidered as
kind-

kindred difpofitions, and forming one habit of the mind] *if it be fuffered to proceed,* &c. Johnfon. *He fent his angels to fight for his people, and the* difcomfiture and flaughter *of great hofts,* is *attributed to their affiftance.*

If the terms be very nearly related, a plural verb is manifeftly harfh ; though it may be thought to be ftrictly grammatical. *His* politenefs and obliging behaviour were *changed.* Hume's Hiftory, vol. 6. p. 14. *was* would have read better. *That quick march of the fpirits, if prolonged, begets a* languor and lethargy, *that* deftroy *all enjoyment.* Hume. *deftroys.*

It is not neceffary that the two fubjects of an affirmation fhould ftand in the very fame conftruction, to require the verb to be in the plural number. If one of them be made to depend upon the other by a connecting particle, it may, in fome cafes, have the fame force, as if it were independent of it. *A long courfe of time,* with *a variety of accidents and circumftances,* are *requifite to produce thofe revolutions.* Hume.

It is very common to confider a collective noun as divided into the parts of which it confifts, and to adapt the conftruction of the fentence to thofe parts,
and

and not to the whole. *If* an academy *should be established for the cultivation of our style, which I, who can never wish to see dependence multiplied, hope the spirit of English liberty will hinder, or destroy*; *let* them, *instead of compiling grammars and dictionaries, endeavour, with all their influence, to stop the licenfe of translators*; *whose idleness and ignorance, if it be suffered to proceed, will reduce us to babble a dialect of French.* Johnson. *Let the members of it* would have been better. In this manner pronouns often mislead persons. Whatever *related to ecclesiastical meetings, matters, and persons*, were *to be ordered according to such directions as the king should send to his privy council.* Hume's History, vol. 8. p. 49. *Can any* person, *on* their *entrance into the world, be fully secure, that they shall not be deceived.* Fair American, vol. 2. p. 26.

It is a rule respecting numbers, that nouns of a singular termination, but of a plural signification, may admit of a verb either singular or plural; but this is by no means arbitrary. We ought to confider whether the term will immediately suggest the idea of the number it represents, or whether it exhibit to the mind the idea of the whole, as one thing. In the

the former cafe, the verb ought to be plural, in the latter it ought to be fingular. Thus it feems harfh to fay with Harvey in Johnfon, *In France the* peafantry goes *bare foot, and the* middle fort, *through all that kingdom,* makes *ufe of wooden fhoes.* It would be better to fay, *The peafantry go bare foot, and the middle fort make ufe,* &c. becaufe the idea, in both thefe cafes, is that of a number. But words expreffing the greateft numbers may be ufed in a fingular conftruction, if the ideas they convey may be conceived at once ; as, *a hundred pounds, a great many men,* &c.

On the contrary, there is an harfhnefs in the following fentences of Hume, in which nouns of number have verbs plural; becaufe the ideas they reprefent feem not to be fufficiently divided, as it were, in the mind. *The* court *of Rome* were *not without folicitude. The* houfe *of commons* were *of fmall weight. The* houfe *of lords* were *fo much influenced by thefe reafons.* Hume's Hiftory, vol. 8. p. 108. *Stephen's* party were *entirely broke up by the captivity of their leader.* Ib. vol. 1. p. 306. *An army of twenty-four thoufand* were *affembled.* One would think that naming the actual number of men, of which
the

the army confifted, would be fufficient to break the idea into its proper parts; but I think that the effect of this fentence upon the ear proves the contrary. An army, though confifting of ever fo many men, is ftill one thing, and the verb ought to be in the fingular number.

Some nouns, however, of a fingular form, but of a plural fignification, conftantly require a plural conftruction; as, *the fewer, or the more* acquaintance *I have. All the* other nobility. *They were carried over to Bohemia by* fome youth *of their nation, who ftudied in Oxford.* Hume's Hiftory.

Other nouns, of a plural form, but of a fingular fignification, require a fingular conftruction; as, mathematicks is *a useful ftudy.* This obfervation will likewife, in fome meafure, vindicate the grammatical propriety of the famous faying of William of Wykeham, Manners maketh *man.*

It is a rule, I believe, in all grammars, that when a verb comes between two nouns, either of which may be underftood as the fubject of the affirmation, that it may agree with either of them; but fome regard muft be had to that which is more naturally the fubject of it, as alfo to that which ftands next to the verb; for if no
regard

regard be paid to thefe circumftances, the conftruction will be harfh. Minced pies was *regarded as a profane and fuperftitious viand by the fectaries.* Hume's Hiftory. A great caufe *of the low ftate of induftry* were *the reftraints put upon it.* Ib. *By this term* was *underftood,* fuch perfons *as invented, or drew up rules for themfelves and the world.*

It feems wrong to join words which are attributes of unity to nouns in the plural number, as the word *whole,* in the following fentences of Mr. Hume. *The feveral places of rendezvous were concerted, and the* whole operations *fixed.* Hiftory, vol. 8. p. 179. *In thefe rigid opinions the* whole fectaries *concurred.* Ib. *Almoft the* whole inhabitants *were prefent.* Ib. This conftruction is, I think, uniformly obferved by this author. Though we fay *a whole nation,* yet there does not feem to be the fame propriety in faying *a whole people.* Hume's Hiftory, vol. 8. p. 92. becaufe the word *people* fuggefts the idea of a number.

It is, and *it was,* are often, after the manner of the French, ufed in a plural conftruction, and by fome of our beft writers. It is *either* a few *great men who decide for the whole, or* it is the rabble *that follow*

follow a feditious ringleader, who is not known, perhaps, to a dozen among them. Hume's Effays, p. 296. It is they *that are the real authors, though the foldiers are the actors of the revolutions.* Lady Montague's Letters, vol. 2. p. 5. It was the hereticks *that first began to rail against the finest of all the arts.* Smollett's Voltaire, vol. 16. 'Tis thefe *that early taint the female foul.* This conftruction feems almoft unavoidable in anfwer to a queftion afked in the fame form. *Who was it that caught the fish?* It was we. This licence in the conftruction of *it is* (if the critical reader will think proper to admit of it at all) has, however, been certainly abufed in the following fentence, which is thereby made a very aukward one. It is *wonderful the very few trifling accidents, which happen not once, perhaps, in feveral years.* Obfervations on the Turks, vol. 2. p. 54.

Alfo, when the particle *there* is prefixed to a verb fingular, a plural nominative may follow without a very fenfible impropriety. There *neceffarily* follows *from thence,* thefe *plain and unqueftionable* confequences.

The word *none* may feem to be a contraction of *no one,* yet it admits of a plural conftruction. *All of them had great authority*

thority, indeed, but none *of them* were *fovereign princes.* Smollett's Voltaire. None *of them except the heir,* are *fuppofed to know them.* Law Tracts, p. 211. This word is alfo found in a fingular conftruction. None *ever* varies *his opinion.* Raffelas, vol. 2. p. 19.

Faults, with refpect to number, are often made by an inattention to the proper meaning of *or* and other disjunctive particles. *Speaking impatiently to fervants,* or *any thing that betrays inattention, or ill humour,* are *alfo criminal* Spectator. *is alfo criminal. A man may fee a metaphor* or *an allegory in a picture,* as *well as read* them *in a defcription.* Addifon on Medals, p. 30. read *it. But their religion,* as well as *their cuftoms, and manners,* were *ftrongely mifreprefented.* Bolingbroke on Hiftory, p. 123. *The author of the infcription,* as well as *thofe who prefided over the reftoration of the fragments,* were *dead.* Condamine's Travels, p. 60.

Words connected with a proper fubject of an affirmation, are apt to miflead a writer, and introduce confufion into the conftruction of his fentences with refpect to number. *I fancy they are thefe kind of gods, which Horace mentions in his allegorical veffel; which was fo broken*

4   *and*

and shattered to pieces. Addison on Medals, p. 74. *The* mechanism *of clocks and watches* were *totally unknown.* Hume. *The* number *of inhabitants* were *not more than four millions.* Smollett's Voltaire. *Let us discuss what relates to* each *particular in* their *order its order.* *There* are a sort *of authors, who scorn to take up with appearances.* Addison on Medals, p. 28.

The word *sort* seems to refer to a number of things, and the word *kind* seems to be more proper when the quality of one single thing is spoken of; yet this distinction has not been observed by writers. *The noblest* sort *of the true critic.* Swift's Tale of a Tub. But allowing that we may say *a sort of a thing*; as *a sort of land, a sort of wheat,* and the like; yet, in this construction, the idea is certainly singular. In the following passage, however, it occurs in the plural number. *There was also among the ancients* a sort of critic, *not distinguished in specie from the former, but in growth or degree; who* seem *to have been only tyro's or junior scholars.* Ib. p. 60.

An endeavour to comprize a great deal in one sentence is often the occasion of a confusion in numbers. *Words consist of* one *or more* syllables; *syllables, of* one *or*

K

more

more letters. One of the moſt aukward of theſe examples I have met with is the following. *The king was petitioned to appoint one, or more, perſon, or perſons.* Macaulay's Hiſtory, vol. *3.*

Many writers, of no ſmall reputation, ſay *you was,* when they are ſpeaking of a ſingle perſon ; but as the word *you* is confeſſedly plural ; the verb, agreeably to the analogy of all languages, ought to be plural too. Beſides, as the verb is in the ſecond perſon, we ought to ſay *you waſt* rather than *you was* ; and, in the preſent tenſe, we always ſay *you are* in the plural number, and not *you art,* or *you is* in the ſingular. *Deſire this paſſionate lover to give you a charaɛter of his miſtreſs, he will tell you, that he is at a loſs for words to deſcribe her charms, and will aſk you ſerionſly, if ever* you was *acquainted with a goddeſs or an angel. If you anſwer that* you never was, *he will then ſay*—Hume's Eſſays, p. 224.

SECTION

SECTION XII.

Of corresponding Particles.

THE greateſt danger of inattention to the rules of grammar is in compound ſentences, when the firſt clauſe is to be connected with two or more ſucceeding ones. There is a prodigious variety of caſes in which this may happen, and the ſtyle of our beſt writers is often extremely faulty in this reſpect. In order to preſerve an eaſy connection of the different clauſes of a ſentence, the ſtricteſt regard muſt be had to thoſe particles, which cuſtom has made to correſpond to one another ; ſo that when one of them is found towards the beginning of a ſentence, the other is expected to follow in ſome ſubſequent part of it. As examples, in theſe caſes eſpecially, are more intelligible than rules, or deſcriptions ; I ſhall produce a conſiderable number of the inſtances of faulty correſpondence, which have occurred to me ; and ſhall inſert, in a different character, the words which would have made them grammatical, or ſubjoin that form of the ſentence, which, I think, would have been better.

Equal is but ill put for *the same,* or *as much,* and made to precede and correspond to *as* in the following sentence. *It is necessary to watch him with* equal *vigour,* as *if he had indulged himself in all the excesses of cruelty.* Hume's History, vol. 6. p. 63. *A girl of twelve cannot possess* equal *discretion to govern the fury of this passion,* as *one who feels not its violence, till she be seventeen or eighteen.* Hume's Essays, p. 286. And *equally* does not well supply the place of *as. This new extreme was* equally *pernicious to the publick peace* as *the others.* Ib. p. 329. *He deems the skirmishes of kites and crows* equally *deserving of a particular narrative,* as *the confused transactions and battles of the Saxon heptarchy.* Ib. vol. 1. p. 28.

The same seems to require *that,* if more than a single noun close the sentence. *Germany ran the same risque as Italy had done.* Bolingbroke on History, vol. 2. p. 180. *The same risque as Italy,* might, perhaps, have done. *She rests herself on a pillow, for* the same *reason* as *the poet often compares an obstinate resolution, or a great firmness of mind, to a rock, that is not to be moved by all the assaults of winds or waves.* Addison on Medals, p. 46. *The highlander has* the same *warlike ideas annexed to the sound found of the bagpipe,* as *an Englishman has to the sound of the trumpet or fife.* Brown. *If I examine the* Ptolemean *and* Copernican *systems, I endeavour only, by my enquiries, to know the real situation of the planets; that is, in other words, I endeavour to give them, in my mind or conception,* the same *relations* as *they bear to each other in the heavens.* Hume's Essays Moral and Political, p. 227.

In the same manner as, or, *in the same manner that,* may perhaps, be equally proper; but the latter construction leans more to the French, and the former is more peculiarly the English idiom. *He told the Queen, that he would submit to her, in* the same manner that *Paul did to Leo.* Hume's History, vol. 5. p. 51.

So does not seem to admit of *as,* when any words intervene between them. *There is nothing so incredible,* as *may not become likely, from the folly and wickedness of John.* Hume's History, vol. 2. p. 100.

So soon as, does not read so well, particularly in the middle of a sentence, as, *as soon as. These motives induced Edward, to intrust the chief part of his government in the hands of ecclesiasticks at the hazard of seeing them disown his authority so soon as it would turn against them.* Ib. vol. 2. p.

422. *Religious zeal made them fly to their standards,* fo foon as *the trumpet was founded by their spiritual and temporal leaders.* Ib. vol. 6. p. 280.

For the reason that is a good correspondence; *for the reason why* is a bad one. For thefe reafons *I fuppofe it is,* why *fome have conceived it would have been very expedient for the publick good of learning, that every true critic, as foon as he had finifhed his tafk affigned, fhould immediately deliver himfelf up to ratfbane or hemp.* Swift's Tale of a Tub, p. 55.

That, in imitation, I fuppofe, of the French idiom is, by Mr. Hume, generally made to follow a comparative. *Such fcenes are* the more *ridiculous,* that *the paffion of James feems not to have contained in it any thing criminal.* Hume's Hiftory, vol. 6. p. 5. *Other princes have repofed themfelves on them with* the more *confidence,* that *the object has been behofden to their bounty for every honour.* Ib. This conjunction is alfo frequently ufed by fome of our more modern writers, in other cafes where the French ufe *que,* and efpecially for *as;* I *never left him,* that *I was not ready to fay to him, dieu vous faffe, &c.* Bolingbroke on Hiftory, vol. 1. p. 121. Perhaps *whtn* would be more truly Englifh in this fen-

sentence, or we should rather say, *I never left him but, or, till I was ready.*

It is a very common fault with many of our writers, to make *such* correspond to *who*; whereas the English idiom is *such as*; and *he, she, they, these,* or, *those. who. It is a place which, for many years, has been much resorted to by* such *of our countrymen, whose fortunes indulge them in that part of education which we call travelling.* Account of Geneva. *A high court of justice was erected for the trial of* such *criminals, whose guilt was the most apparent.* Hume's History, vol. 7. p. 289. *those criminals.*

Scarce, or *scarcely,* does not admit of *than* after it. Scarcely *had he received the homage of this new pontiff,* than *John the twelfth had the courage to stir up the Romans again.* Smollett's Voltaire. There is a much better correspondence to this particle in the following sentence, from the same author. Scarce *had he left the camp,* when *the very same night, one half of the emperor's army went over to his son Lotharius.*

When two clauses of a sentence require each a different particle, it is very common to forget the construction of the former clause, and to adhere to that of the

the latter only. *He was* more *beloved, but not so much admired* as *Cinthio.* Addifon on Medals. *More* requires *than* after it, which is no where found in this fentence. *The fupreme head of the church was a foreign potentate, who was guided by interefts always* different, *fometimes contrary* to *thofe of the community.* Hume's Hift. vol. 4. p. 35. *Never was man fo teized, or fuffered* half the uneafinefs as *I have done this evening.* Tatler, N° 160. The firft and third claufe, viz. *Never was man fo teized as I have been this evening,* may be joined without any impropriety ; but to connect the fecond and third, *that* muft be fubftituted inftead of *as,* and the fentence be read thus ; *or fuffered half the uneafinefs* that *I have done,* or elfe, *half fo much uneafinefs as I have done.*

Negative particles often occafion embarrafment to a writer, who, in this cafe, is not fo apt to attend to the exact correfpondence of the different parts of a fentence. *Nor is danger ever apprehended in fuch a government from the violence of the fovereign,* no more *than we commonly apprehend danger from thunder or earthquakes.* Hume's Effays, p. 133. *any more. Ariofto Taffo, Galileo,* no more than *Raphael,* were

not

not *born in republicks.* Hume. *Neither*
certainly requires *nor* in the clauſe of a
ſentence correſponding to it. *There is ano-*
ther uſe that, in my opinion, contributes ra-
ther to make a man learned than wſe, and is
neither *capable of pleaſing the underſtanding,*
or *imagination.* Addiſon on Medals, p.
16. *No* does but ill ſupply the place of
neither in this correſpondence. *Northum-*
berland took an oath, befoi e two archbiſhops,
that no *contraƐt, nor promiſe had ever poſ-*
ſed between them. Hume's Hiſtory, vol.
4. p. 174. *or promiſe.*

Never ſo was formerly uſed where we
now ſay *ever ſo.* This form is generally
to be found in the works of Mr. Addiſon,
and others of his age. It is conſtantly
uſed in our tranſlation of the Bible. *Charm*
he never ſo *wiſely.*

The comparative degree and the conjunction *but* have not an eaſy correſpondence. *Than* is preferable. *The miniſter*
gained nothing farther *by this,* but *only to*
engage the houſe to join the queſtion of the
children's marriage with that of the ſettlement
of the crown. Hume's Hiſt. vol. 5. p. 105.
Beſides does not ſtand well in the ſame
conſtruction. *The barons had little* more
to rely on, beſides *the power of their fa-*
milies.

milies. Hume's Hiftory, vol. 2. p. 193. *more than,* or take away the word *more* and the conftruction will be more eafy. Neither does *befides* follow in correfpondence with *other* near fo well as *than.* *Never did any eftablifhed power receive fo ftrong a declaration of its ufurpation and invalidity; and from no* other *inftitution,* befides *the admirable one of juries, could be expected this magnanimous effort.* Hume's Hiftory, vol. 7. p. 209. Nor does *but* do fo well as *than.* *They had no* other *element* but *wars.* Ib. vol. 1. p. 104.

THE END

For EU product safety concerns, contact us at Calle de José Abascal, 56–1°,
28003 Madrid, Spain or eugpsr@cambridge.org.

 www.ingramcontent.com/pod-product-compliance
Ingram Content Group UK Ltd.
Pitfield, Milton Keynes, MK11 3LW, UK
UKHW010336140625
459647UK00010B/635